WORDS
THAT SHAPED
OUR WORLD

VOLUME TWO

SOUND WISDOM BOOKS BY JIM STOVALL

Words That Shaped Our World 1 (with Kathy Johnson)
Words That Shaped Our World 2 (with Kathy Johnson)
The Ultimate Gift
The Ultimate Life
The Ultimate Journey
The Ultimate Legacy
The Millionaire Map
The Ultimate Financial Plan
Ultimate Hindsight
The Gift of a Legacy
A Christmas Snow
Success Secrets of Super Achievers
Today's the Day!
The Art of Learning and Self-Development
The Art of Productivity
The Art of Presentation
The Art of Communication
The Financial Crossroads
Ultimate Productivity
Keeper of the Flame
The Lamp
Poems, Quotes, and Things to Think About
Wisdom of the Ages
Discovering Joye
Top of the Hill
One Season of Hope
Wisdom for Winners Volumes 1, 2, 3, 4
100 Worst Employees
The Will to Win
The Art of Entrepreneurship
Passport to Success (with Dr. Greg Reid)

WORDS THAT SHAPED OUR WORLD

QUOTES THAT CHANGED HOW WE THINK, WHAT WE DO, AND WHO WE ARE

VOLUME TWO

LEGENDARY VOICES OF HISTORY

JIM STOVALL & KATHY JOHNSON

Published and distributed by:
SOUND WISDOM
P.O. Box 310
Shippensburg, PA 17257-0310
717-530-2122
info@soundwisdom.com
www.soundwisdom.com

While efforts have been made to verify information contained in this publication, neither the author nor the publisher assumes any responsibility for errors, inaccuracies, or omissions. While this publication is chock-full of useful, practical information; it is not intended to be legal or accounting advice. All readers are advised to seek competent lawyers and accountants to follow laws and regulations that may apply to specific situations. The reader of this publication assumes responsibility for the use of the information. The author and publisher assume no responsibility or liability whatsoever on the behalf of the reader of this publication.

ISBN 13 TP: 978-1-64095-497-7

ISBN 13 eBook: 978-1-64095-498-4

For Worldwide Distribution, Printed in the U.S.A.

1 2 3 4 5 6 7 8 / 28 27 26 25 24

DEDICATION

The authors dedicate this book to the publishers, editors, booksellers, and librarians who create, perfect, and present the written word. These people record our history, preserve our thoughts, and make our world a bigger and better place.

CONTENTS

INTRODUCTIONS

Jim Stovall and Kathy Johnson

FIRST, I WANT TO THANK YOU for the investment of time and money you have made in this book. In the world today, both time and money are in short supply, and I never take it for granted that my readers choose one of my books when there is a multitude of new titles being offered in the marketplace every day.

I have written more than 50 books to date, and each of them is special to me in different ways and for different reasons. Whether it's a novel or a nonfiction title, there are books that, when you write the last page, you are well aware that the subject has been covered or the story has been told. There are other books that, when you write the last page, you have a deep awareness of the fact that, while this project may be complete, there is much more the characters have to say, or there have been details uncovered about the topic that need to be addressed.

When my colleague, coauthor, and friend Kathy Johnson and I wrote the first volume of *Words That Shaped Our World*, it was an amazing experience. Once we completed the final chapter in that book, we both agreed that we had barely scratched the surface of the great quotes that have been spoken or written throughout history. As often happens when we are confronted with a bit of knowledge or wisdom, it may fill an immediate need, but can also create a hunger and launch a quest for more.

In this second volume, we want to build on the foundation of the first book, exploring the context of quotations from world leaders, business icons, and adored entertainers. All of the quotes in this book, and the previous title, are readily available to anyone who wants to take the time and make the effort to look them up. What is not easily accessible is the background of the person who gave us the quote and the context of the point in history and cultural environment in which the quote was presented.

My coauthor, Kathy Johnson, has once again done a masterful job in providing the research that makes each of these powerful quotes come to life. In the first volume of *Words That Shaped Our World*, we presented a quote from one of my favorite authors, Louis L'Amour, who said, "No one can be judged except by the backdrop of the time and place in which they lived."

Within these pages, you will encounter some of the most powerful words ever spoken or written. But more importantly, you will understand what was going on in the world at that time as well as how each of the quotes can apply to you and me here in the 21st century. While we are excited to share powerful quotes with you that changed the world when they were presented, we are more excited that, when fully understood, these same quotes can change your world now and in the future.

—Jim Stovall, 2023

In this, our second volume of Words That Shaped Our World, my dear friend and collaborator, Jim Stovall, and I bring you another assortment of personalities as told through their unique quotes and inspiring stories. Our selection includes entrepreneurs, celebrities, sports figures, comedians, artists, musicians, authors, and even the first man to walk on the moon.

Though many of the people you will read about lived in an era ahead of my time and yours, they are all influencers in the modern world. Each of them, in their own way, has shared a unique style of character, some modest and humble, others with hubris and pride that has withstood the test of time. Through their individuality and distinct personalities, we have come to appreciate their one-of-a-kind superpowers that shaped how we view the world.

From Henry Ford to Andy Rooney and everyone in between, their thought-provoking quotes encourage us to believe that our dreams can become a reality. We have not traveled to distant planets or explored the depths of the oceans, and we were not there to design the Model T, but we laughed with Lucille Ball, Steve Martin, and Mel Brooks and still enjoy the moving tunes of John Lennon.

In the marked words of Michael Jordan, he notes, "Some people want it to happen, some wish it would happen, others make it happen."

Featured within these pages are people who had a vision and made their dreams come true through diligence and hard work—sometimes with a comedic flair and sometimes by merely being in the right place at the right time to offer their exemplary talents. They are genuine people who turned their gifts outward to share with others.

In my research, I came to appreciate those spotlighted within and found that while they have done extraordinary things, they are no different from you or me.

They had a vision and followed their dreams.

—Kathy Johnson, 2023

1

*"It is my observations that most people get
ahead during the time others waste time."*

HENRY FORD

HENRY FORD was born the eldest of five children on July 30, 1863,
and grew up on a prosperous farm in Dearborn, Michigan. His
father, William Ford, was born in County Cork, Ireland, and
immigrated to Michigan, where he met Henry Ford's mother, Mary
Litogot Ford, of Belgian descent. He became an American automobile manufacturer, industrialist, entrepreneur, founder of the Ford
Motor Company, and chief developer of the assembly line technique of mass production, commonly known as "Fordism." Fordism
is a method of producing an automobile in one-tenth of the time
previously required for its manufacture. In addition, he created the
first automobile affordable for middle-class Americans. As a result
of his ingenuity, the Ford Motor Company has sold more than 4.2
million cars worldwide. Over time, Henry Ford amused himself by
dabbling in shipbuilding, home construction, rubber painting in
Brazil, radio broadcasting, soybean farming, and aviation.

As a young man, Henry Ford was mechanically minded and
an innovator at heart. At 12, he fashioned a small machine shop

for himself, where he spent much of his idle time tinkering away. In that same little workshop, Henry Ford constructed his first steam engine.

By age 15, he found satisfaction in dismantling and reassembling timepieces for friends and neighbors. He first experimented on a pocket watch his father gave him. His ability to craft and restore timepieces soon affirmed his reputation as a watch repairman. When he determined he needed a tool not accessible to him, he merely created one to fit his needs.

Henry Ford's father had dreams of his son taking over the family farm one day, but at 16, the young man left the farm and settled in Detroit, Michigan, where he became a machinist's apprentice. Three years after leaving home, he returned to the family farm and continued operating and servicing steam engines.

Though he never liked living on the farm, he once wrote, "I never had any particular love for the farm—it was the mother on the farm I loved." Henry Ford's mother died in 1876, leaving the 13-year-old devastated.

In 1888, he married Clara Bryant, who had also grown up on a nearby farm, and in 1891, Henry Ford returned to Detroit with his bride and took a job as an engineer with the Edison Illuminating Company. He quickly rose through the ranks. Within two years, Henry Ford was the company's chief engineer. During that time, Clara gave birth to the couple's only child, a son they named Edsel Bryant Ford, on November 6, 1893.

The company had put Henry Ford on call 24 hours a day, seven days a week. The irregular hours gave him ample time to develop and perfect a horseless, gasoline-powered carriage he called the "Ford Quadricycle."

Completed in June 1896, Henry Ford's first gasoline engine came to life in the shed behind his home at 58 Bagley Avenue in Detroit, Michigan. It was an automobile with a buggy seat consisting of a light metal frame made from angle iron structured in a cross-section to form an "L" shape and four large bicycle wheels to support it. A leather belt and chain drove the transmission, and it was powered by a two-cylinder, four-horsepower gasoline engine driven by the back wheels. It was a design that laid the foundation for future automobiles.

In 1903, Henry Ford expanded his production of the automobile. He followed through the alphabet, naming his first version the "Model A." Some of his automobiles were brought to market briefly or as limited editions, and some remained only prototypes. Five years later, he reached his most successful version—the Model T. The Model T was simple to drive, inexpensive to repair, and initially cost the consumer $825. In today's currency, it would cost less than $24,000. Henry Ford proved that middle-class Americans could purchase their own automobiles.

While he may not have been the first to develop a gasoline-powered engine, Henry Ford was the first to create an economical method for mass-producing his automobiles. Eventually, this time-saving approach led to the Ford Motor Company turning out a Model T every 24 seconds, and he changed American transportation forever.

In his autobiography, Ford wrote, "Any customer can have a car painted any color that he wants, so long as it is black." Fortunately for the consumer, once the assembly line approach was developed, black paint was no longer mandated merely because of its quicker drying time. From that time forward, the Model T was available in other colors, including red.

Consequently, Henry Ford's "assembly line" concept made it possible for various companies that adopted his method to become more effective and efficient and bring their products to market much faster.

In a surprising move in 1914, Henry Ford astonished the world by increasing all his employees' wages. For some, their wages doubled. He raised the salaries of his factory workers from $2.34 a day to $5.00 per day—approximately $130 per day in today's terms. This gesture reduced turnover, raised productivity, lowered the company's overall training costs, and nearly cornered the employee market. In addition, he reduced the workweek to five days. These modifications attracted highly skilled workers and made the Ford Motor Company an attractive company to work for. The wage increases also made his cars affordable to employees, significantly boosting the economy.

Wisely, Henry Ford offered his socially worthy employees a share of his $10,000,000 in profits. Profit-sharing was provided to all employees with sixty months of service or more who conducted themselves in a manner that the Ford Motor Company's "Social Department" affirmed. Employees were not permitted to consume alcohol heavily, gamble, or become deadbeat dads. A team of 50 investigators monitored employees to ensure they met Ford standards. Not surprisingly, a large percentage of employees qualified for profit-sharing.

Believing in quality above all else, Henry Ford insisted that his name connoted a commitment to hard work, impeccable ethics, compassion for others, and a desire to improve society through his leadership. As a leader, he served rather than be served.

In 1923, Henry Ford received a letter that intrigued him. It read: "We want to build an all-metal airplane. If you join us, it will cost you one thousand dollars, and for your thousand, you get one promise—you will never get your money back," signed William B. Stout, Inventor.

Henry Ford and his son, Edsel, each invested $1,000, and the Stout Model Airplane Company perfected an all-metal air transport named "Air Pullman." It had a spacious cabin with sleeping berths and a galley. Their investment paid off, and in 1925, Henry Ford purchased the company, determined to increase passenger safety and elevate operating revenue. He renamed the entity the Ford Airplane Manufacturing Division and initiated the development of a three-motor airliner.

Unfortunately, by 1933, the economy experienced the effects of the Depression (1929 to 1939). Henry Ford sensed a need to concentrate on his automotive industry and withdrew from aviation. Some say he never had the passion for airplanes as he did for automobiles.

In 1918, at 55, Henry Ford resigned as president of Ford Motor Company. His son Edsel was elected president in his absence in January 1919 and remained its top executive until he died of cancer in May 1943. Then, at nearly 80 years old, Henry Ford rejoined the company. Once again, he was its president, albeit briefly, before handing it over to his grandson, Henry Ford II, in 1945.

Long past Edsel Ford's death, the "Edsel" model Ford was introduced to the market. From 1957 to 1960, only 118,287 were sold. Sorrowfully, Edsel Ford never saw the car named in his honor.

Henry Ford died at his home in Dearborn, Michigan, on April 7, 1947, at age 83. He once stated that he attributed his success to three things, "He had no fear of the future, held no veneration for the past, and put service before profit."

Today, the Henry Ford Museum of American Innovation, Greenfield Village, and Edison Institute is visited by more than 1.7 million people each year. The museum holds priceless collections, such as the presidential limousine of John F. Kennedy, Abraham Lincoln's chair from Ford's Theatre, Thomas Alva Edison's laboratory, the Wright Brothers' bicycle shop, the Rosa Parks bus, and many other historical exhibits. It has been named the largest indoor/outdoor museum complex in the United States.

When I was asked to appear in the *Think and Grow Rich, The Legacy* movie to provide my commentary on the life of Napoleon Hill, I was excited to learn that the film project would feature re-enactments about some of the most successful innovators of all time—including Thomas Edison, Guglielmo Marconi, and Henry Ford.

The Ford segment of the movie highlighted a time in his life when the *Chicago Tribune* printed a front page story declaring that Henry Ford was an ignorant man who had succeeded more through luck than talent or knowledge. As the movie portrays, Ford sued the newspaper and prevailed in court by demonstrating knowledge and wisdom are not the act of memorizing countless obscure facts, but instead knowledge and wisdom come when we learn where to obtain information and can access it when we most need it.

In his quote, Ford points out that we all have the same amount of time, and we can get ahead as we leverage knowledge and information applying it in the form of wisdom.

2

"For every action there is always opposed an equal reaction."

SIR ISAAC NEWTON

SIR ISAAC NEWTON was born December 25, 1642, or January 4, 1643, at Woolsthorpe Manor in Woolsthorpe-by-Colsterworth, a hamlet in Lincolnshire, England. Curiously, he was born at a time in history when the Julian calendar, the Roman calendar proposed by Julius Caesar in 46 BC, and the Gregorian calendar, implemented in October 1582 by Pope Gregory XIII, were both recognized.

The adoption of the Gregorian calendar, which the world accepts as a standard today, modified and replaced the Julian calendar to more closely coincide with the "tropical" or "solar" year that determines Earth's rotation around the sun. This adjustment changed the New Year from March 25 to January 1. The difference in days between the calendars was ten days at Sir Isaac Newton's birth and had progressed to eleven days at his death. Legal documents of the era reflected both dates, and Sir Isaac Newton's existence was dually recorded in history.

The Englishman, who spoke many languages, including English, Latin, and Greek, was considered the greatest mathematician and physicist. He was a well-respected astronomer, theologian, scholar, and noted author. He was referred to as a "natural philosopher" in the philosophical study of nature. Widely revered in his lifetime, Newton was both a scientist and politician.

In 1705, at age 63, Queen Anne conferred knighthood upon him. He was not honored for his mathematics and scientific accomplishment, but rather, the distinction was bestowed for his political work as the president or head of the Royal Society of London. He presided over meetings of the society's council.

Sir Isaac Newton faced many challenges in his early life. Three months before he was born, his father, a prosperous local farmer also named Isaac, died. The infant joined the world prematurely but was not expected to live. His mother purportedly once said that he was so small at birth that he could fit inside a quart mug. Tiny and weak, he managed to survive.

When he was three, Sir Isaac Newton's mother, Hannah Ayscough, remarried a financially secure minister leaving the young boy to be raised by his maternal grandmother. This abandonment had a profound effect on the lad. He developed insecurities and lacked communication and social skills. At 12, still bitter toward his mother for leaving, she reemerged into his life when her second husband died, bringing three small children back to Woolsthorpe Manor with her.

Some speculate that due to his profound powers of concentration, underdeveloped social skills, above-average intelligence, and other related traits, Sir Isaac Newton suffered from a form of high-functioning autism, commonly known as Asperger's syndrome. Over time, he rigorously obsessed over his published work, sometimes with irrational behavior.

Despite Sir Isaac Newton's challenging start in life, he made many contributions to the world of science and mathematics. Fundamentally, his contribution included "Newton's theory of gravity," the quantification of gravitational attraction, and "Newton's theory of color," the discovery that when observed through a spectrum or prism, white light is a mixture of invariable spectral colors rather than the object generating colors themselves. In 1665, he originated the formation of a mathematical binomial theorem that later became known as "calculus." In addition to these observations and discoveries, he was known to involve himself in the discipline of alchemy, or as termed in seventeenth-century England, "chymistry."

After graduating with a Bachelor of Arts degree in 1665 from Trinity College, Cambridge, where he eventually became a professor, the institution closed for a time due to the Great Plague of London, also known as the bubonic plague. It forced him to return to the family farm. During his eighteen-month hiatus as a student, he conceived many of his most significant observations.

At this time legend has it that Sir Isaac Newton experienced his most notable and inspiring theory relating to gravity. While sitting beneath an apple tree, he witnessed an apple fall straight—rather than at an angle—to the ground, reportedly hitting his head, as the myth goes. A question bound to his mind, "Why may not this power extend to the moon, and then what more would be necessary to retain her in her orbit about the earth?"

In his mind, the concept of uniform and accelerated motion led to his theory that all mass gravitates to the Earth's core, precipitating accelerated velocity. He deduced that if the moon were without a doubt held to Earth by earthlike gravity, the planets moving around the sun might similarly be retained in their orbits by gravity toward Earth. He further theorized, "So then gravity may put the planets into motion, but without the Divine Power, it could never put them into such a circulating motion, as they have about the Sun."

Sir Isaac Newton published many of his theories and writings throughout his lifetime. In 1687, he published *Philosophiae Naturalis Principia Mathematics*, translated *Mathematical Principles of Natural Philosophy*. It is often referred to as the *"Principia"* and is considered the most influential book on physics. It offers three basic laws of motion: "A stationary body will stay stationary unless an external force is applied to it; Force is equal to mass times acceleration, and a change in motion is proportional to the force applied; and For every action, there is an equal and opposite reaction." While this publication is available in reprint today, a 1726 third edition, the last edition edited by Sir Isaac Newton himself, can be found on the Internet selling for a mere $32,000, plus tax.

Today, Sir Isaac Newton's known writings on alchemy, titled *The Chymistry of Isaac Newton,* are being developed online in a project undertaken by Indiana University in Bloomington, Indiana.

Sir Isaac Newton lived his final years with his step-niece Catherine Barton in London. He had devoted his life to work, never marrying or having children. On March 20, 1726 (Old Style calendar—Julian) or March 31, 1727 (New Style calendar—Gregorian), he died in his sleep at age 84. He was honored by a ceremonial funeral attended by nobles, scientists, and philosophers. He was buried in Westminster Abbey among kings and queens, famous writer Charles Dickens, naturalist and geologist Charles Darwin, and Henry VIII's fourth wife, Anne of Cleves. He was the first scientist buried at the Abbey.

After his death, Sir Isaac Newton's hair was examined. It contained the chemical element mercury, perhaps resulting from his exposure to its water-soluble form or by ingesting or inhaling its vapor from his alchemical pursuits. Mercury poisoning could have impacted his further eccentricities as he aged.

As an author, speaker, movie producer, and columnist in the field of success and personal development, I've always been amazed at how many of Sir Isaac Newton's observations about the physical world around us mirror how we can succeed or fail in our personal or professional lives.

Newton's theory of inertia, which explains that bodies in motion tend to stay in motion, while bodies at rest tend to remain at rest, speaks to us all as we strive to improve who we are and how we change the world around us. Once you've achieved a degree of success, it becomes easy and natural to build on that success as you continue to excel. But if you find yourself stuck at a point in life where you're not making progress, one of the most difficult things you will ever do is to start moving and get into action.

From Newton's quote about the laws of motion, we can interpret it as we all have choices and each of those decisions comes with consequences; as well as the fact that life is not as much about what happens to us as it is about what we do about what happens to us.

3

"Life is what happens while you are busy making other plans."

JOHN LENNON

BORN OCTOBER 9, 1940, JOHN WINSTON LENNON, later calling himself John Winston Ono Lennon after his marriage to Yoko Ono, began life in the relatively poor northwest port city of Liverpool, England. His father, Alfred "Alf," was a seafaring man, not present in his son's life. When John Lennon was five, he went to live with his aunt, Mary Elizabeth "Mimi" Smith. She lived in a posh area of England and had no children. His mother, Julia, found it challenging to support her son alone. So, reluctantly, she permitted her sister to raise him. "Mum" was only a bus ride away.

Not believing his claim that he would be famous one day, Mimi did not support Lennon's musical aspirations. She hoped he would tire of the notion, claiming, "The guitar's all very well, John, but you'll never make a living at it." She was equally dismissive of his girlfriends and wives.

To Aunt Mimi's delight, the British singer, songwriter, musician, and peace activist launched pinnacle success as the founder, co-songwriter, co-lead vocalist, rhythm guitarist, and electric pianist of the legendary Beatles rock band in 1960.

The group included John Lennon, Paul McCartney, singing co-lead and guitarist, George Harrison on lead guitar, and Ringo Starr (Richard Starkey) on drums. The band drove the youth of America into a wild frenzy. The Beatles, the first band to write their own songs—lyrics *and* music thanks to the duo of Lennon-Mc-Cartney—became a pop sensation, creating the "British Invasion" phenomenon in the United States known as Beatlemania.

Wherever the boys went, scores of screaming girls of all ages pushed through crowds for a chance to touch one of them or score a souvenir. The boys stopped wearing scarves in cold weather to avoid losing them to fanatics or the risk of strangulation. While they were on stage, fans cried real tears, fainted, and swooned as though the boys in the band were singing exclusively to each of them.

The Beatles' sound was influenced by the combined musical stylings of rock and roll, skittle, a genre of folk music motivated by blues and jazz, and American traditional pop music of the 1950s. Their debut single, "Love Me Do," hit the charts in England on October 5, 1962, and their first number-one hit in the United States was "I Want to Hold Your Hand," released on December 26, 1963. John Lennon never doubted that his group of talented musicians was exceptional from the start—first in their community and later around the globe. But he never imagined the band's overwhelming impact on popular music culture.

The Beatles undeniably influenced the fashion world with their custom-made Pierre Cardin's Edwardian collarless suitcoats, matching slim trousers, skinny ties, and heeled black Chelsea boots. Under manager Brian Epstein's direction in 1962, the group's style evolved from its "teddy boy" image of tight leather suits, cowboy boots, sideburns framing their faces, and greased-back hairstyle that came together to resemble the feathers of a duck's tail to a unique clean-cut style. Epstein believed no record company would take the band seriously if they did not change their image. The boys' new bobbed hairstyle, known as the "mop-top," started a worldwide fashion trend. The combed-forward hairdo became the mod youth style of the 1960s. "I remember so vividly showing up at a show, and you'd be in your ordinary clothes," Lennon said. "And then you'd take out of your little suitcase your suit and your shirt and put them on. And then finally your 'Beatle boots,' and you'd stand up, and you just looked at each other like 'yeah, there we are.'"

Sadly, in 1967, the band transformed their iconic look after Epstein died of an accidental drug overdose. They grew their hair long, wore beards and mustaches, and dressed in bright, bold colors.

John Lennon's mother was a high-spirited and astute banjo player. She taught her son to play simple chords on the banjo. Subsequently, he tuned his Gallotone Champion acoustic guitar similarly. The first song he learned to play was Fats Domino's "Ain't That a Shame." Later, he learned proper guitar chords and moved away from banjo-style playing.

In late 1956, before the group became the Beatles, Lennon, then 16, assembled a band of several musical schoolmates from his Quarry Bank High School in Liverpool. Initially, they took the name "Black-jacks" before discovering another group already called themselves by that label. The group soon renamed the band "Quarrymen."

The story of John Lennon cannot be told fittingly without recounting how John met Paul and the pair became one of the most successful songwriting duets in history.

On July 6, 1957, the Quarrymen played an event in a field under the clear blue skies at the Woolton Saint Peter's Church fete. Ivan "Ivy" Vaughan, a friend of Lennon's, invited his school pal James "Paul" McCartney to listen to the band play. Lennon captivated McCartney when he heard him play the little-known song "Come Go With Me," recorded by the 1950s doo-wop musical group The Del Vikings. He cleverly improvised the words, not proficient in the song's lyrics.

As the band awaited their on-stage performance inside the church later that day, McCartney boldly asked for a "go" on Lennon's guitar. After perfectly re-tuning it, McCartney turned it upside down and played it left-handed. He performed Eddie Cochran's hit, "Twenty Flight Rock." Impressed with McCartney's talent, Lennon asked him to join the band within two weeks. The pair soon began their journey of writing songs and making music together.

In February 1958, McCartney invited his friend, George Harrison, to watch the band perform. Harrison, then only 14, gave an excellent audition, but Lennon felt he was a bit young for the group. With fierce persistence, Harrison delivered a stellar instrumental performance of "Raunchy" on lead guitar atop the upper deck of a Liverpool bus. That day, he earned his spot as lead guitarist.

One year later, in January 1959, all of Lennon's Quarry Bank High School friends left the band, leaving Lennon, McCartney, and Harrison to the rhythms of the all-guitar band.

By then, Lennon had enrolled in the Liverpool College of Art, majoring in various artistic disciplines, including painting, sculpture, and graphic design, and changed the group's name to "Johnny and the Moondogs."

In 1960, Lennon invited friend and fellow student Stuart Sutcliffe, a painter who had just sold one of his art pieces, to join the band, provided he agreed to purchase a bass guitar. The group played rock and roll whenever they could find a drummer to sit in and play with them.

Eventually, they hired Randolph "Peter" Best. Sutcliffe, not fond of the band's name, suggested the group change it to "Beatals" as a play on the pioneering figure of mid-1950s rock and roll, Buddy Holly's insect-inspired band, "Buddy Holly and the Crickets." In May, they became the "Silver Beetles," changing the spelling from Beatals, and toured Scotland as the backup group for pop singer Johnny Gentle. Again, refashioning themselves, they later became known as the "Beatles," with a whole new spelling.

In August 1962, the Beatles got their first recording contract. Believing that Peter Best's personality did not blend well with the group, Epstein fired him, and the contract went to the band's substitute drummer, Ringo Starr.

In 1970, after working together for ten years, the Beatles' relationship began to deteriorate. Many speculate it was due to Lennon's drug use and his relationship with his second wife, Yoko Ono, who fashioned herself as the voice of John Lennon. Others believed it was because McCartney wanted to branch out and perform solo. No matter, the breakup was a blow to the music industry and the band's loyal fans.

In 1975, after performing solo since the breakup, Lennon took a five-year hiatus from the music industry to devote his full attention to his second son, Sean Taro Ono Lennon.

John Lennon demonstrated a rebellious nature and sharp wit throughout his life, expressing it in his music, writings, drawings, and non-violent protests. His relationship with Ono brought national attention with his staged demonstrations, including the famous "Bed-in," where he and Ono protested against worldwide violence from their honeymoon bed. Lennon once said, "When it gets down to having to use violence, then you are playing the system's game. The establishment will irritate you—pull your beard, flick your face—to make you fight. Because once they've got you violent, then they know how to handle you. The only thing they don't know how to handle is non-violence and humor."

Sadly, on December 8, 1980, any hope of the "Fab Four," as the group was often called, ever reuniting vanished. The one-time *de facto* leader of the Beatles, John Lennon, was gunned down by Mark David Chapman as he and Ono returned to The Dakota apartments in New York City, New York. At 5:00 that evening, the soon-to-be gunman stopped the couple while leaving their apartment for an autograph on their recently released album, *Double Fantasy*. Chapman was again waiting upon their return from *The Record Plant* recording studio around 10:50 p.m. He called out to Lennon as he walked through the building archway and pulled the trigger five times—John Lennon was hit four times in the back and shoulder at close range. For his crime, Chapman pleaded guilty to second-degree murder and received a 20-years-to-life prison sentence. According to parole board records, Chapman has been denied parole twelve times due to his action leaving "the world recovering from the void which he created." He remains in solitary confinement for his own safety from adoring Lennon fans.

Leaving The Record Plant that fateful evening, Lennon spoke to Ono for the last time. "I said, 'Shall we go and have dinner before we go home?'" she recalled, "And John said, 'No, let's go home because I want to see Sean before he goes to sleep." Sean was five at the time.

Lennon left behind two sons—John Charles "Julian" Lennon, born in 1963, with Cynthia "Cyn" Lennon, his first wife of ten years, and Sean Taro Ono Lennon, born on Lennon's 35th birthday in 1975, whom he shared with Ono. Both men possess musical talents like their father.

John Lennon wrote the 1967 song "Strawberry Fields Forever" in memory of his childhood experiences when he used to play in the garden of a children's home that the Salvation Army ran in Woolton, a suburb of Liverpool. The home was called "Strawberry Fields." After Lennon's cremation, Ono scattered his ashes in New York City's Central Park, near the "Strawberry Fields" memorial built in his honor.

Shortly before his death, in a September 1980 interview, John Lennon recalled his family and his rebellious nature: "A part of me would like to be accepted by all facets of society and *not* be this loudmouthed lunatic poet/musician. But I cannot be what I am not...I was the one who all the other boys' parents—including Paul's father—would say, 'Keep away from him.' The parents instinctively recognized I was a troublemaker, meaning I did not conform, and I would influence their children, which I did. I did my best to disrupt every friend's home. Partly out of envy that I didn't have this so-called home...but I *did*."

The Beatles received many honors during and after their fame. In 1965, the "Fab Four" was awarded the prestigious royal MBE granted by Queen Elizabeth II, making each a "Member of the Order of the British," the third-highest ranking honor—knighthood being the highest—for "amazing achievement and service to their country." In time, the royal order knighted Sir James Paul McCartney (knighted in 1997) and Sir Richard Starkey (knighted in March 2018).

On November 25, 1969, as John Lennon progressed deeper into his peace and activism movement, he returned his MBE medal to Queen Elizabeth II in protest, writing, *"Your Majesty, I am returning the MBE as a protest against Britain's involvement in the Nigeria-Biafra thing, against our support of America in Vietnam, and against 'Cold Turkey' slipping down the charts. With love, John Lennon of Bag."*

The song mentioned, "Cold Turkey," was written and performed by John Lennon in 1969 and drew on his and Ono's experience of abruptly quitting their drug addiction. The signature, "John Lennon of Bag," referenced Lennon and Ono's creation of *Bagism* as a peaceful protest to satirize prejudice and stereotyping. It involved genuinely wearing a "bag" of sorts over one's entire body.

In 1988, the band was inducted into the Rock and Roll Hall of Fame. It came eight years after the death of John Lennon. As of 2022, the Beatles have sold more than 600 million music units worldwide, becoming the best-selling musical artist of all time.

John Lennon took risks in his personal life and his career. Beyond his physical life, his soul remains in his music, drawings, and writings.

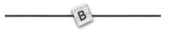

I grew up in a home where we had a monaural record player that was the size of a modern day washing machine. We had a stack of 33 1/3 RPM vinyl albums that were mostly gospel and big band music, so I was surprised when, as a five-year-old, my parents let me stay up far past my bedtime one Sunday night to watch the Ed Sullivan Show with them. It was the Beatles' first appearance on television in America, and it changed our culture forever.

The Beatles burst onto the scene in America a few short months after the tragic assassination of John F. Kennedy and the end of that era commonly known as Camelot. America was ready for something new, exciting, and fun. The Beatles and John Lennon certainly fit the bill. The Lennon and McCartney creative collaboration reminds us all that when you connect with the right people, it doesn't add, it multiplies. One plus one can equal ten or even a hundred in the mathematics of success.

I will always remember coming into my dorm room late one night as a junior in college and hearing on the news that John Lennon had been killed. I felt like a huge part of my childhood and a creative force in the world was gone forever. Now that I understand the power of legacy, I realize that John Lennon's contributions to the world, just like yours and mine, will never die.

4

"Courage is being scared to death and saddling up anyway."

JOHN WAYNE

JOHN WAYNE was born Marion Robert Morrison on May 26, 1907, in Winterset, Iowa, weighing in at a whopping 13 pounds. Though he alleged his parents later changed his middle name to Michael to give the name Robert to their second son, no legal documents have been discovered to confirm his claim. As a boy, he adopted the nickname "Duke."

In 1916, the family moved to Glendale, California. Wherever he went, he had his huge Airedale Terrier named Duke by his side. On his way to school each day, he passed the local fire station. Knowing his big dog was Duke, one fireman dubbed Morrison "Little Duke." Not much liking the name "Marion," he preferred the more strapping sound of Duke. Over time, the iconic Westerns and war movie legend stood 6' 4" tall, and "little" no longer applied, but the name stuck with him throughout his life.

Duke Morrison grew to become one of America's most iconic film stars and filmmakers, famously known as "John Wayne." He appeared in 179 film and television productions. As John Wayne, he was a tough, self-confident, iconic Western cowboy figure with steely gray-blue eyes and a swagger to his walk. He wore a wide-brimmed Stetson hat with a front-pinched, diamond-creased crown, and he used the same 1873 Colt Single Action Army revolver in many Western pictures.

He consistently played the rugged good guy role in his films, bringing something unique to fight scenes early in his career by matching the bad guy's fighting style. Convincingly, he paralleled their brutality to his good-guy approach, still winning the audience's favor. "Before I came along," John Wayne said, "It was standard practice that the hero must always fight clean. The heavy was allowed to hit the hero in the head with a chair or throw a kerosene lamp at him or kick him in the stomach, but the hero could only knock the villain down politely and then wait until he rose. I changed all that. I threw chairs and lamps. I fought hard, and I fought dirty. I fought to win."

Though he did not achieve the highest marks in school, Morrison was skilled in academics and sports. He played high school football, competed on the debate team, served as president of the Latin Society, and contributed to the sports column of the school newspaper. He liked to body-surf in the ocean in his spare time, riding the waves face down in the water with his arms stretched, allowing the waves to take him toward the shore. It was a sport that changed the course of his life.

Upon graduation from high school in 1925, he applied to the United States Naval Academy but was rejected because his grades were not good enough. Instead, he attended the University of Southern California (USC) in Los Angeles on a football scholarship and majored in pre-law. Morrison played offensive tackle for the Trojans under Coach Howard Jones and was a Trojan Knight and Sigma Chi fraternity member. Though his scholarship paid his tuition and one meal a day, he needed pocket money while attending college. So, he and a few of his teammates worked part-time at Fox Film Corporation as stuntmen, moving studio furniture, serving as prop boys, and appearing as extras in films.

As a sophomore at USC, his future careers in law and football were shattered when he broke his collarbone in a body-surfing accident. Powerless to play the game, his scholarship was revoked. Unable to pay for his education, he was forced to withdraw. He took up more duties at the Fox Film Corporation and performed in minor roles due to his financial situation. His on-screen credits listed him as "Duke Morrison" in only one 1929 film titled, *Words and Music*.

In 1930, Director Raoul Walsh cast him in his first starring role in *The Big Trail*. He suggested Marion Morrison be renamed Anthony Wayne after the Revolutionary War General "Mad" Anthony Wayne. Film producer Winfield Sheehan was not fond of the name. He believed it sounded ethnically Italian and suggested "John Wayne." At that moment, John Wayne's name changed without his presence or input. Though he was known on-screen as John Wayne, he remained the "The Duke" to his devoted fans.

John Wayne's 40-year acting career spanned from the silent film era of the 1920s through the Golden Age of Hollywood, making his last film in 1979. He exuded integrity, intelligence, and determination in every motion picture and was considered one of the top box office draws for three decades.

In the 1933 film *Riders of Destiny*, at age 26, Wayne became Singin' Sandy, only the second singing cowboy of the time—the first being Ken Maynard in the 1929 Western film *The Wagon Master*. Unfortunately, Wayne was not a talented singer, so the studio mandated that his voice be dubbed with a more suitable vocalist. The actual singer was Bill Bradbury, the son of the film's writer and director, Robert N. Bradbury. Later, the studio abandoned the idea that Wayne sings in his movies for two reasons. First, he could not accommodate children who clamored for a Singin' Sandy song from the film, and second, Bill Bradbury's voice did not resemble Wayne's. Gene Autry was selected as Wayne's replacement in the newly adopted singing cowboy genre.

As he appeared in more Westerns, stunt performers mentored him to improve his horseback riding skills and Western persona.

Wayne starred in many genres, including Westerns, drama, action, comedy, romance, and war films. Some of his more popular titles include *Fort Apache* (1948), *Sands of Iwo Jima* (1949), *Rio Grande* (1950), *The Quiet Man* (1952), *Rio Bravo* (1959), *The Alamo and Liberty Valance* (1960), *McClintock!* and *Donovan's Reef* (1963), *In Harm's Way* and *Sons of Katie Elder* (1965), *The Green Berets* (1968), and *True Grit* (1969), for which he won an Academy Award Oscar for "Best Actor."

Though traditionally a Western film icon, in support of the war at a tumultuous time in history when Hollywood was reluctant to do so, Wayne produced and starred as Colonel Mike Kirby in the Vietnam-era film *The Green Berets*. Admirers of "The Duke" may remember the trademark golden brass bracelet he wore on his right wrist in his movies. It was a gift he received while filming *The Green Berets*, and it remained one of his most treasured possessions. Wayne was never spotted—on-screen or off—without it.

In the summer of 1967, while filming *The Green Berets,* Wayne spent time with the indigenous native Montagnard People of Vietnam's Central Highlands. They were known as the Degar and shared much in common with Wayne, including a decisive fight against communism. The Montagnards gifted him the bracelet to signify their friendship, and he wore it for the remainder of his life. It represented acceptance and respect, and he became an honorary member of the Montagnard People. It is said that it meant so much to him that he was laid to rest wearing it.

John Wayne was a cigarette chain smoker beginning at an early age. Subsequently, he was diagnosed with lung cancer in 1964. Doctors surgically removed his left lung and two ribs to save his life. Though his business associates did not want him to go public with his illness, believing it would result in him losing film roles in future projects, he publicly announced his disease. He encouraged people to seek preventative examinations. In 1969, he was deemed cancer-free. It was John Wayne who coined the term "Big C" as a euphemism for cancer.

In his final film, *The Shootist,* released in 1976, he portrayed an aging gunfighter dying of cancer. Ironically, he, too, suffered another bout of the disease. On June 11, 1979, John Wayne died of stomach cancer at the UCLA Medical Center.

The Duke had married three times and left behind seven children, several of whom followed in their father's footsteps by entering the entertainment business.

John Wayne was buried at Pacific View Memorial Park in Newport Beach, California. His grave is located near the ocean, where he spent much of his free time sailing on his yacht, the *Wild Goose.*

It was a decommissioned United States Navy YMS-1-class Yard Mine Sweeper built in Ballard, Washington. The large vessel was listed in 2011 on the U.S. National Register of Historic Places.

His final resting place remained unmarked for 20 years after his death to preserve his gravesite from spectators and to respect other families with loved ones buried nearby. In 1999, his family had a change of heart and decided to memorialize his grave with a plaque that reads:

Tomorrow is the most important thing in life.

Comes into us at midnight very clean.

It's perfect when it arrives, and it puts itself in our hands.

It hopes we've learned something from yesterday.

JOHN WAYNE 1907 – 1979

In an interview, his son Ethan Wayne said, "I personally think it's wonderful that people want to go see him. He was a public person. He had a relationship with his family. But he also had a relationship with his fans. His fans allowed him to lead his lifestyle...He spent probably three to four hours a day just answering fan mail. Every letter got answered. They like him. If they want to go see him, I think it's wonderful. He had a tremendous impact on people."

John Wayne remains a classic American cinema icon.

I spend a lot of my time writing books and syndicated columns, making movies, and giving speeches, but my foundation business that I launched more than 30 years ago is Narrative Television Network. NTN makes movies and TV shows accessible to millions of blind and visually impaired Americans and countless others around the world. When we first started the company, we broadcast a lot of classic films from the golden age of motion pictures. In order to fit time formats for satellite distribution, I hosted a talk show and interviewed many of the classic film stars in our movies to round out the available time.

One of the movies we ran in our first season on national television was a 1947 Western titled, *Angel and the Bad Man* starring John Wayne. Since Mr. Wayne had already passed away, I sought and received comments from two other movie stars—Katharine Hepburn and Jimmy Stewart—about their experiences working with John Wayne.

Katharine Hepburn, who was John Wayne's costar in *Rooster Cogburn,* explained that he was not a great actor, but he was one of the greatest movie stars of all time. She felt that John Wayne always portrayed himself on the screen and found roles that fit his persona. Within those unforgettable characters, he became an enduring star.

Jimmy Stewart worked with John Wayne in his last movie, *The Shootist.* Mr. Stewart played a doctor who diagnosed John Wayne's character's terminal cancer and described how the disease would progress. Jimmy Stewart may have put it best when he told me that a 40-foot theater screen dwarfed most actors, but always seemed just right for John Wayne.

5

"I came, I saw, I conquered."

JULIUS CAESAR

GAIUS "JULIUS" CAESAR (Latin pronunciation, "Iulius Kaiser"), born July 13, 100 BC, was a charismatic Roman statesman with a genius for persuasion and oration. He was a brilliant military and political leader, strategist, risk-taker, public speaker, and member of the "First Triumvirate," or informal alliance established in 60 BC. The coalition consisted of three prominent politicians— Gnaeus Pompeius Magnus, Marcus Licinius Crassus, and Julius Caesar. Though often rivals, the trio formed a secret collaboration to sidestep the checks and balances established by the constitution of the Roman Republic. The constitution was designed to prevent one individual man from rising above all others to create a monarchy.

In his final years, Julius Caesar became the Dictator of Rome from 49 BC until his assassination in 44 BC. He began the events that led to the fall of the Roman Republic, transforming it into the Roman Empire. As an accomplished author and historian, accounts, albeit biased, of his personal life and military battles were well documented in his writings.

Historian Adrian Goldsworthy wrote of Julius Caesar, "He was a politician and statesman who eventually took supreme power in the Roman Republic and made himself a monarch in every practical respect, although he never took the name king."

Julius Caesar was a tall, balding man with a fair complexion, a broad face, and dark eyes. He was born into a wealthy family with a noble lineage. His father, also named Gaius, was not notably influential, but many of his ancestors had held esteemed positions in the Roman Republic. At age 16, Caesar's father died. It was a time when Rome had descended into near anarchy, and it was time for him to set sail to the Isle of Rhodes to study oratory.

Along his journey, Caesar was kidnapped for ransom by barbarous pirates. While his ransom was being arranged, he entertained himself by writing poems and bold speeches, which he read aloud only to be received by the crew's mockery and insults. The pirates chalked up his behavior as youthful nonsense. In return, the irritated Julius Caesar spiritedly called them illiterate barbarians and vowed to kill them all upon his release. Regrettably, they did not take the boy's threat to heart. Once his ransom was paid and the pirates released him, Julius Caesar immediately assembled vessels from the harbor of Miletus (current-day Turkey) to retaliate against the bandits. As promised, he crucified them all.

As an army commander clad in his blood-red cloak, Caesar fought alongside his men from 58 BC to 50 BC against tribes opposing Roman rule. His forces successfully expanded Roman territory. He waged wars for trade and riches, defeating the Gallic army led by Vercingetorix, the king and tribal chief of the Arverni people, in 52 BC. Julius Caesar rose to become one of the most powerful military leaders of his time.

When the Gallic Wars concluded, the Roman Republic Senate ordered him to step down from his military command, disband his army, and return to Rome. Sensing that the Senate had his demise in store, he defied their authority, crossed the shallow Rubicon River that served as a boundary between Rome and its provinces, marched toward Rome, and reemerged with his mighty army. A civil war ensued against Republican forces. Victoriously, Julius Caesar assumed control of the government. Though the Senate and the elite men were unhappy, the people loved him.

Still in the wages of a civil war with the Roman Republic, Caesar arrived in the Mediterranean port city of Alexandria, Egypt, in 48 BC while pursuing his military enemy, Gnaeus Pompeius Magnus, known as "Pompey the Great." There, he met Greek-Egyptian Queen Cleopatra, who was at odds with her rebellious brother, who was also her husband, and Co-regent Ptolemy XIII for sole power of Egypt. Cleopatra arranged a meeting with Julius Caesar to gain support and settle the dispute, which led to a victory for Cleopatra.

From that meeting in 49 BC, Caesar and Cleopatra began an adulterous relationship that did not end until his death and produced a son, Ptolemy XV Caesar, in August 47 BC. They called him "Caesarion." In January of the same year, newly pregnant with Julius Caesar's child, Cleopatra's husband, Ptolemy XIII, drowned in the Nile River while fleeing the city. She immediately married her younger brother, Ptolemy XIV, to ensure her reign in Egypt.

Throughout the affair, Julius Caesar was married to his fourth wife, Calpurnia, who was a meek, submissive, and mannerly woman, unlike the bold personality of Cleopatra. It is noted that Caesar had adulterous relationships with multiple women, and his reputation as a philanderer was well-known throughout Rome.

Julius Caesar's power enabled him to grant citizenship to residents from foreign regions, initiate land reform and support for veterans, and proclaim himself "Dictator for Life." As Dictator, Caesar began social and government reforms, such as creating the Julian calendar, adopted to replace the Roman calendar, in 45 BC. The calendar had fallen more than two months behind the natural year. With help from Cleopatra's astronomer, Caesar created the Julian calendar to realign the error. The system was then comprised of 365 days and accounted for the leap year.

The Roman Republic was transforming into the Roman Empire. With time, Caesar's popularity and authoritarian reforms riled his political opponents so much that 60 Senators conspired against him, claiming Julius Caesar's unprecedented concentration of power undermined the Roman Republic and deemed his behavior an act of tyranny.

In 44 BC, on March 15, the first new moon of the month, etched historically as the infamous "Ides of March," Caesar was brutally stabbed 23 times. The attack was carried out by the rebellious group of Senators led by Marcus Junius Brutus, son of Servilia, with whom Caesar, despite his marriage to his first wife, Cornelia, had a passionate and long-term affair, and Gaius "Cassius" Longinus, Brutus' brother-in-law. A new series of civil wars broke out, and the Republic was never fully restored. Though there is no proof, it has been said that Julius Caesar said nothing at all during his attack. It was English playwright William Shakespeare who penned his final words. In his stage play, *Julius Caesar*, performed in 1599, he wrote that Caesar's last words were "et tu, Brute?" translated to "You too, Brutus?"

Ultimately, his assassination had the opposite effect on the citizens of Rome than his executioners had envisioned. The people were appalled by Julius Caesar's ruthless murder and demonstrated their loyalty. Five days after his death, in his honor, they threw personal items and extra wood onto his cremation fire as his body burned in the public forum. The additional fuel raised the flames high into the sky, signifying his greatness.

Marc Antony, his friend, colleague, and consul, used Caesar's last wishes to further invoke fury within the citizens of Rome against the Senators and conspirators responsible for his death. In his public speech, he recalled the good deeds of Julius Caesar and the brutal stabbing at the hands of the Senators, falling short of calling them by name. Marc Antony shared that Julius Caesar left his gardens as a park to the city of Rome and gave every citizen a large amount of money. Caesar also proclaimed the adoption of his grandnephew, Octavian, as his son in his will.

While precisely what Marc Antony said may not be known, it incited a fiercely angry mob. Mourners raised an effigy of Julius Caesar that resembled his lifeless body that lay before them. There were 23 stab wounds on the dummy's body and face. Openly, they showed their hatred for the Senators by reeling the Roman Republic wildly toward civil war. The crowd surrounded the Senate house with howling cries and burnt it to the ground. Meanwhile, the murderers had fled the city they sought to liberate.

A denarius depicting Julius Caesar's image was minted two months after his death. On the coin's reverse was the goddess Venus holding a scepter. Experts claim that there are only three such coins that remain today.

Julius Caesar's name will forever be synonymous with the title "Emperor." He was the first Roman to be deified officially, and he was granted the title *Divus Iulius* or "Devine Julius" by decree of the Roman Senate on January 1, 42 BC. A comet seen in the sky during the Roman religious festival and games in his honor served as confirmation to the people of Rome of his deity.

To this day, visitors can tour the exact location in Rome where Julius Caesar met his tragic death by assassination. Though it is dedicated in his honor, it has also become a sanctuary for cats.

Julius Caesar lived a large life. Whether he was conquering in battle, struggling in his personal life, or dealing with his political rivals, he did nothing on a small scale. It's hard to know how much of Julius Caesar's story is myth, legend, or history. Whether it's epic novelists, Hollywood producers, or no less a talent than William Shakespeare, throughout the centuries we have experienced the best and worst of humanity through the life of Julius Caesar.

I will always remember him as crossing the Rubicon, which was both a symbolic and real-life point of no return. If we are going to conquer in life, we must be willing to go beyond our own personal Rubicon and stake our very existence in the cause of success.

6

"I want to stand as close to the edge as I can without going over. Out on the edge you see all the kinds of things you cannot see from the center."

KURT VONNEGUT

BORN NOVEMBER 11, 1922, IN INDIANAPOLIS, INDIANA, KURT VONNEGUT JR., the youngest of three children, was an American playwright, essayist, and novelist. He is considered one of the most influential novelists of the twentieth century. His works are routinely examined in high schools, colleges, and universities throughout the country, for his literary approach and wry humor. His culturally barbed writing style combined satirical science fiction elements and cynical wit and humor, sometimes angled toward the absurd. He created unique worlds and one-of-a-kind characters.

With a career that spanned 50 years, Kurt Vonnegut published fourteen novels, three short story collections, five plays, and five non-fiction works. He liked to interject relatable hand drawings between the pages of his books. He wrote classics such as *Player Piano*, his first novel in 1952, *Cat's Cradle*, *Breakfast of Champions*, and his most famous, *Slaughterhouse-Five*, to name a few. When *Slaughterhouse-Five* was released, it hit the top of the charts casting him onto *The New York Times* bestseller list. He received countless invitations from his success to give speeches, lectures, book readings, and commencement addresses.

In Kurt Vonnegut's 1982 novel, *Deadeye Dick*, he takes a satirical look at the death of innocence. Through his narrator's eyes, he saw life as a story, saying, "We all see our lives as stories, it seems to me, and I am convinced that psychologists and sociologists and historians, and so on, would find it useful to acknowledge that. If a person survives an ordinary span of 60 years or more, there is every chance that his or her life as a shapely story has ended and that all that remains to be experienced is epilogue. Life is not over, but the story is."

His father, Kurt Vonnegut Sr., was an architect with Vonnegut & Bohn in Indianapolis. In the 1930s, Prohibition and the economic depression significantly impacted Americans' pocketbooks. Work was hard to find, and for Vonnegut Sr., his services were not in demand, as there was not much money for public or private development. Over time, he became demoralized and surrendered to a deep depression. He had become grumpy and melancholy, and as Kurt Vonnegut said of his father, "He was in the state of embarrassment when I knew him."

Kurt Vonnegut's mother, Edith, was a highly intelligent woman of culture, and he considered her a good writer. She was heir to the family-owned Lieber Brewery. During the Great Depression, the business went bankrupt, creating a more significant financial strain on the family. Once independently wealthy, the economy's fall had a devastating effect on her mental health and stability.

His parents spoke German but did not teach their three fourth-generation German-heritage children the language. Perhaps it was due to the anti-German attitudes they carried with them post-World War I and its destabilization. For Vonnegut, the family's disaffection with his heritage gave him a feeling of cultural displacement and a sense of rootlessness that he lugged around throughout his life.

Once financially affluent, when the Great Depression was at its height, the family lost their wealth, was forced to sell their home, relocated to a rental house, and moved their children from a private to a public school in 1936—Shortridge High School, Indianapolis' oldest free public high school. Vonnegut believed the public school system and its attentive teachers enriched his education and lent substance to his writing talents. While attending, he played the clarinet in the school band and became coeditor of the Tuesday edition of *The Shortridge Echo* newspaper. He enjoyed writing for the large student body, finding it "fun and easy," he said. "It just turned out that I could write better than a lot of other people. Each person has something he can do easily and can't imagine why everybody else has so much trouble doing it."

Growing up in a society he believed thought scientists, engineers, and mathematicians should run the world because of their logical thinking and common sense, Vonnegut enrolled at Cornell University, Ithaca, New York, in 1941 to study physics, mathematics, and chemistry. After a couple of years, he found he was flunking his classes, so he dropped out—never graduating. It was the height of World War II, and he decided to join the United States Army. The Army sent him to study engineering at Carnegie Technical Schools, now called Carnegie Mellon University, in Pittsburgh, Pennsylvania, in 1943.

On leave from the military in 1944, Vonnegut and his sister, Alice, found their mother, Edith, had succumbed to her many nervous breakdowns by committing suicide from an overdose of barbiturates the night before Mother's Day. Life, as the family knew it, changed. "I only wish she'd lived to see my writing career. I only wish she'd lived to see all of her grandchildren," he said of his mother's suicide. "Suicide solves everything, but it punishes the living." Later in life, he told his daughter, Nanette, "The reason you mustn't consider suicide is because you leave that legacy to the next generation. You give *them* a reason to do it."

Kurt Vonnegut served in the 106th Infantry Division in Europe during the Battle of the Bulge in Dresden, Germany. German forces captured him and many other Americans on December 19, 1944, and he spent long, laborious hours in an underground meat locker making vitamins. He said sneeringly, writing of his unit's situation, "Bayonets aren't much good against tanks." At night, the POWs slept in an underground slaughterhouse—Slaughterhouse-Five—with unsanitary conditions, sadistic guards, and meager food rations.

From February 13 to 15, 1945, allied forces, the British Royal Air Force and United States Army Air Forces, conducted air raids that destroyed more than 1,600 acres of Dresden and completely devastated the beautiful and cultured city. Though Vonnegut and his comrades who worked alongside him escaped harm, nearly 25,000 civilian men, women, and children were buried alive where they stood. In a *Paris Review* interview, Vonnegut said, "One hundred thirty-eight corpses were hidden underground. It was a terribly elaborate Easter egg hunt." When the bombing ceased, the German army forced their prisoners to locate and remove the jewelry and other valuables from the dead in the heap of ruins before torching their bodies.

Vonnegut and other POWs were liberated by their captors in May 1945. Even today, nearly 45 percent of the stonework structures of Dresden cast a burnished black hue by the catastrophic firestorm. For those who survived, the experience continued to plague their memories.

Later that year, Vonnegut was discharged from the Army due to frostbite. He received a Purple Heart. It was his experience in Dresden that he wrote his bestselling novel, *Slaughterhouse-Five*, two decades later in 1969. He expanded the science fiction, anti-war novel's title to *Slaughterhouse-Five, or The Children's Crusade: A Duty-Dance with Death*, because, in effect, wars are fought by young men—still babies.

When he returned from his tour of duty in 1945, Kurt Vonnegut and his childhood sweetheart, Jane, whom he had met in kindergarten, married. The newlyweds moved to Chicago and enrolled at the University of Chicago. He entered as an Anthropology student on his G.I. Bill, combined his undergraduate and graduate programs, and was granted a master's degree.

The couple had three biological children. When their first son was born, a great admirer of Mark Twain, the couple named him Mark—Vonnegut then grew his iconic Mark Twain mustache. When his sister, Alice, died of cancer in 1958 and her husband died in a train wreck thirty-six hours earlier, Vonnegut and his wife adopted their three young boys.

The harsh realization of life, the profound effect of losing his mother, and the loss of the American dream as a child manifested itself in the theme of many of Kurt Vonnegut's writings. He painted mental imagery of skepticism, disillusionment, and dismal societies that many readers in the 1960s could relate to in his works. His character, notably Kilgore Trout, an unsuccessful science-fiction writer who came into view in four of his novels, was, admittedly, his alter ego.

Kurt Vonnegut died on April 11, 2007, at age 84, from a head injury he sustained when he fell down the steps of his New York City brownstone, with his second wife, photographer Jill Krementz and their adopted daughter, Lily, by his side. Those who know him will remember him as a free spirit who loved to laugh—admittedly, when he was both happy and sad, and often at inappropriate times—sometimes turning laughter into a cough and wheeze from his lifelong relationship with "Pall Mall" cigarettes. "Laughter is just like crying very often," he said. "With laughter, there's less clean-up afterward."

Vonnegut received many prestigious honors. In 2015, he was inducted into the *Science Fiction and Fantasy Hall of Fame*. The asteroid "25399" and a crater on Mercury are named in his honor. The *Kurt Vonnegut Museum and Library* in Indianapolis, Indiana, opened in 2010 and was designated a Literary Landmark in 2021. The library battles censorship by giving free copies of *Slaughterhouse-Five* to students whose schools have banned the book. His slogan, "So it goes," was a recurring refrain from that novel, meaning, "Such is life." His achievements are showcased, including signed copies of his books and literary rejection letters. Visitors can view his drawings, family photos, typewriter, cigarettes (Pall Mall, of course), and his Purple Heart.

In 2007, Lev Grossman of the *New York Times* summed up Kurt Vonnegut by saying, "Vonnegut's sincerity, his willingness to scoff at received wisdom, is such that reading his work for the first time gives one the sense that everything else is rank hypocrisy. His opinion of human nature was low, and that low opinion applied to his heroes and his villains alike—he was endlessly disappointed in humanity and himself, and he expressed that disappointment in a mixture of tar-black humor and deep despair. He could easily have become a crank, but he was too smart; he could have become a cynic, but there was something tender in his nature that he could never quite suppress; he could have become a bore, but even at his most despairing he had an endless willingness to entertain his readers: with drawings, jokes, sex, bizarre plot twists, science fiction, whatever it took."

Kurt Vonnegut wrote short, quick chapters, and each ended with a precisely devised page-turner. He had a minimalist, dry style that made his writing seem simplistic. But "so it goes," it takes a stroke of genius to achieve success.

Every writer of my generation owes a debt of gratitude to the masters whose work we learned from. Kurt Vonnegut impacted my generation of authors. I've written more than 50 books and a good number of them are novels. However, I believe the only true fiction is fantasy or science fiction. Many of us create characters and put them into familiar situations within the world we know. Kurt Vonnegut created new worlds with characters living unheard of lives so that readers can understand our world and our lives better. I don't always agree with Kurt Vonnegut's perspective when I read his work in books, plays, or essays, but he never fails to make me think.

In his quote at the beginning of this chapter, he describes viewing the world while standing on the edge. That perspective allows the rest of us to go beyond what Kurt Vonnegut wrote and really get in touch with our own thoughts.

7

"The two most powerful warriors are patience and time."

LEO TOLSTOY

ONE OF THE MOST NOTABLE AUTHORS, Count Lev Nikolayevich Tolstoy, also known in English as Leo Tolstoy, was born on August 28, 1828, of Russian nobility, in Tula Province, Russia. He was the fourth of five children and became one of the world's leading philosophers, writers, crusaders for humanity, and the Russian people's prophet and moral conscience. He wrote novels, stories, and poetry and kept numerous diaries published after his death.

Among the finest and lengthiest of novels ever written were his two most noted masterpieces, *War and Peace,* completed in 1869 when he was 41, and *Anna Karenina*, 1877. His writings aimed to guide readers to understand his dislikeable characters and know that no one should be outside the circle of sympathy and forgiveness, for no one is all good or all bad.

Tolstoy did not intend his novels to be enjoyed solely for entertainment but as a tool for psychological education and reform. They must attempt to educate about emotional health and ethical good sense. He believed that such a medium would be a way to encourage his readers to expand their humanity and tolerance toward others.

In his novella, *The Death of Ivan Ilyich*, Tolstoy's message is conveyed through a high-court Russian judge who must come to terms with his relationships and his own death. It examines the consequences of living a life without meaning.

Traditionally, persons of nobility, such as Tolstoy, master many languages—he was no exception. He was fluent in Russian, English, French, and German and could read seven other languages. He had collected approximately 23,000 books written in 39 languages in his library.

Leo Tolstoy's father was Count Nikolai Ilyich Tolstoy, a veteran of the Patriotic War of 1812, and his mother was Countess Maria Tolstaya. She died giving birth to a daughter when Tolstoy was merely two years old. His father died seven years later, leaving the 9-year-old to be raised by relatives—first his grandmother until her death and then an aunt who lived in Kazan. Until his father's death, the family lived on his mother's ancestral country estate in the village of Vasnaya Polyana, located 130 miles south of Moscow. It would become his home on and off for the rest of his life.

A large 32-room mansion stood on thousands of acres of land with picturesque hills among the dense forests. Three hundred and fifty peasant serfs worked the estate and lived in a cluster of four houses. In those days, Russian serfs were the property of the land and not owned by landowners. As children, Leo Tolstoy and his siblings swam and bathed in the ponds—four in all—in the summer and ice skating on them in the winter. Tolstoy's older brother, Nikolai, claimed to have hidden a little green stick somewhere on the estate and told his younger brother that carved upon the side of it was a secret. Should the secret ever become known, a golden age would descend upon the earth, and all misery and evil would cease. He said the person who finds the magic wand would never die or become ill, and men would live as brothers. Tolstoy spent hours upon hours searching for that green stick. He never found it.

Leo Tolstoy entered the University of Kazan in 1844, beginning his studies in the philosophy department before transferring to law a year later. He had failed many of his courses, and one of his lecturers claimed he was "unable and unwilling to learn." Finding no interest in school and having inherited the family estate, he withdrew from the university at age 19.

With his departure from Kazan, he returned to Vasnaya Polyana and began living a leisurely yet rogue life. He spent much of his time in pubs and bars in Tula, St. Petersburg, and Moscow, excessively gambling, drinking, and partying with Moscow gypsies and other free-spirited women. By 1851, Tolstoy had racked up significant gambling debts and lost his family's mansion in a card game. The new owner dismantled, moved, and later demolished the home.

After several years, Tolstoy had tired of the superficial life and rowdiness. In his diary he described his misspent youth, "I fought duels to slay others, I lost at cards, wasted the substance wrung from the sweat of peasants, punished the latter cruelly, and deceived men. Lying, robbery, drunkenness, violence, murder—all committed by me, not one crime omitted."

Leaving the frivolous life behind, Tolstoy joined the army as an artillery officer, fought alongside his brother in the Crimean War, and began writing. His first novel, *Childhood,* published in 1852, was a collection of memories inspired by his childhood and appeared in the Russian magazine *Contemporary.* He wrote many stories about his experiences in the war. By 1956, he was a well-known author.

In the 1860s, his life took on a new direction. In 1862, 34-year-old Tolstoy married 18-year-old Sofya Andreyevna Behrs, whom he called Sonya. The daughter of a court physician, she was intelligent, sophisticated, and highly cultured. The couple had thirteen children—nine survived infancies—and they educated them at home. They lived comfortably on the Vasnaya Polyana estate in a large white house near the original mansion.

Once settled into his family life, Tolstoy grew a beard to the middle of his chest. He became obsessed with fitness and hard work. He walked about barefoot, mainly, and joined in the daily chores of the peasants, working alongside them.

In a documentary, his daughter Alexandra, whom he called Sasha, said that, occasionally, her father played with her and her younger brother, dragging them about the room on a carpet as they joyfully hung on. Sometimes, he put them in a large basket. He carried the basket to a dark corner and asked the children, as she recounted the experience in her native dialect, "Well, guess where are you?" Perhaps his interaction with his children was infrequent, for Tolstoy once wrote that he found his children "so repulsive, pathetic, and degrading to listen to...it would have been better for me to have no children at all."

Leo Tolstoy divided his day into quads—before breakfast, he devoted the hours to physical labor by clearing snow from the courtyard and cutting wood for their ten warming stoves. After breakfast, he concentrated his mind on writing until lunchtime. When finished with lunch, his activities turned to agile workmanship and artisan labor until dinner, and afterward, he spent time with his family and guests. They talked, played music, and enjoyed games of chess.

Over time, Tolstoy rejected authority, strongly promoted human rights, rejected violence, and disassociated himself from all organizations identifying with the Russian Orthodox Church and State. For this, he was excommunicated and marked as a traitor, resulting in mounting tension in his marriage but increasing his following worldwide. In his work, Leo Tolstoy turned from what he called "irresponsible fiction" and began writing about more spiritual and ethical issues. His stance on asceticism set his marriage spiraling even more. He vowed to live by a code of ethics that promoted non-violence, universal love, and forgiveness, and he opted for a simpler lifestyle.

He began wearing peasant rags, never deviating from his iconic white belted tunic and boots that he made himself. He freed his serfs, renounced his title as Count, gave money to peasants, built schools for Russian peasants, became a vegetarian, and promoted progressive education. Despite his wife's opposition, Tolstoy attempted to give his estate to people experiencing poverty, and he wanted to place his works in the public domain for "all people of the world." His wife adamantly objected, saying he must care for his children financially. In the end, Sonya was granted all financial benefits for his writings before 1880. All revenue received for works after 1880 was donated to charity.

Leo Tolstoy's teachings extended worldwide and, most notably, to Mahatma Gandhi, whom he influenced through their correspondence. His advice to the young lawyer regarding his homeland of India was, "Do not participate in evil—in violent deeds of the administration, in the law courts, the collection of taxes, and what is more important, in soldiering, and no one in the world will enslave you."

Tolstoy's marriage to Sonya continued to be difficult, with significant quarrels erupting frequently. There was bitterness stemming from both sides. Sonya was a jealous wife and grew increasingly irritable with her husband. Tolstoy complained that they had entirely opposing ideas of the meaning of existence. He wrote in his diary, "I feel I must save myself—what is inside me that may be still useful to people." The "inside" he spoke of was his spirituality, and he believed his family life was stifling.

In later years, Leo Tolstoy suffered from rheumatism, toothaches, intestinal enteritis, and spells of weakness. In 1902, he contracted malaria, a lung infection, and typhoid, and six years later, he suffered a series of minor strokes and developed phlebitis, causing pain throughout his body. The aging man's eyesight deteriorated, but he refused to wear glasses. His vision became so bad that he sawed the legs of his desk chair to only 17 inches high so that his chin was a mere seven inches from his desktop as he wrote.

Leo Tolstoy contemplated leaving Vasnaya Polyana and his family many times to escape his wife's tirades, for she had disapproved of many of his beliefs. In the early hours of October 28, 1910, he woke to find Sonya in his study rifling through his papers, became furious, and decided to leave his wife of 48 years. Her behavior had taxed his health and strength, and he wrote, "She does not even need my love. She needs only one thing—that people should think I love her. This is what is so dreadful."

That night he went to Alexandra's room, as she recalled in an interview in 1970, "Suddenly, there was a knock at the door, and he came in with a little lantern. He said things." She listened to his reasons for deserting the family, and finally, he said, "Now you understand. I'm leaving altogether."

On the bitterly cold night, the 80-year-old Tolstoy went to the stables dressed only in his lightweight peasant clothes. With Alexandra's help and that of the stable's coachman, he climbed atop his horse and secretively rode off through the orchard. He rode as far as the Astapovo railway station intending to buy a third-class ticket bound for the Russian border. The long horseback ride through the wintery night took its toll, and he contracted pneumonia. Sequestered, he remained in the train master's modest apartment with his physician. The Russian press recorded every detail, including images of Sonya peeking through the closed window to catch a glimpse of her dying husband. She was not permitted inside for fear that it would cause sudden death for Tolstoy.

Leo Tolstoy died less than a month later, on November 20, 1910. Throughout his life, he wrote five wills, with the final shortly before his death. Defying his wife's desires, he left all of his writings, diaries, and copyrights to Alexandra with the directive that she gives everything "to the people." Obeying her father's last wishes, she bought the family estate from her mother and brothers and turned Vasnaya Polyana over to the peasants.

In his will, he stated that he wished to be buried in the small clearing near a ravine that he and his brother called "the place of the green wand." Known as the "Forest of the Old Order," it was a part of the forest preserve since his grandfather's time, and tree cutting was forbidden. Many were more than one hundred years old.

Thousands of peasants and Tolstoyan followers from all parts of Russia lined the streets at his funeral. On the shoulders of many strong men, the casket carrying Tolstoy's body was paraded back to Vasnaya Polyana. It was a public event. The police tried diligently to limit access to the procession. Even those who merely knew that "some nobleman had died" came from miles around.

The world mourned his death, and his daughter, Alexandra, was overcome with emotion as tears streamed down her cheeks. A close friend reminded her of what her father once said and believed, "Life is a dream; death is an awakening." She cried for him no more.

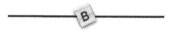

Of the 50 books I've written, approximately two dozen are novels—eight of which have been turned into movies. I'm always looking for great characters and great plots. I've often said the key to outstanding fiction is creating compelling characters who do engaging things. Few authors have ever done this as well as Leo Tolstoy. He mastered the art of creating realistic characters.

When one writes fiction, there is the temptation to make the good characters perfect and the bad characters totally evil. In reality, we are all a compilation of both. Tolstoy created complex characters who endured throughout his epic novels.

In Tolstoy's quote at the start of this chapter, he reminds us that patience and time are the tools we have to build our future. Tolstoy could have been among the most compelling characters to ever appear in his own novels.

8

"I'd rather regret the things I've done than regret the things I haven't done."

LUCILLE BALL

LUCILLE DESIRÉE BALL was an American movie and television actress, model, producer, television production studio owner, and stage talent. She was all those things, but she will always be remembered as the zany slapstick comedian from her long-running situation comedy program, *I Love Lucy*, where she starred alongside her on and off-screen husband. The show aired from 1951 to 1957 and has never been off-programming. It continues to be broadcast in syndication more than seventy years later.

Lucille began her career in 1929 as a model and cast member for small parts in low-budget B movies but ended it as the *Lucy* everyone still loves today. Throughout her career, she appeared in more than 70 motion pictures. Her talent earned her great recognition, and she was nominated for 13 Primetime Emmy Awards—winning five. Other notable accolades include the Golden Globe Cecil B. DeMille Award for "outstanding contributions to the world of entertainment" and the Kennedy Center Honors given to individuals in the performing arts for their lifetime contribution to

American culture. Lucille Ball was inducted into the first-ever Television Hall of Fame in 1984. On the Hollywood Walk of Fame, she has two stars—one for her contribution as a television star and one for her success in motion pictures.

On August 6, 1911, Lucille Ball was born in Jamestown, New York, to Henry Durrell "Had" Ball, an electrical lineman for the Bell Telephone Company, and Desiree "Dede" Eveline Hunt Ball. Henry's job frequently required the family to relocate around the country—Montana, New Jersey, and ultimately, Wyandotte, Michigan.

When Lucille was four, she lost her 27-year-old father to typhoid fever, so she never had the opportunity to get to know him. After his death, the family moved back to Jamestown to live with Dede's parents. At the time, Dede was expecting their second child, Frederick "Fred" Henry Ball. Without her dad, Lucille looked to her grandfather as a father figure.

Four years later, Dede married Edward "Ed" Peterson and moved to Detroit with him as he looked for work. She left Fred with her parents, and Lucille lived with Ed's parents. Lucille spoke of the Petersons as having little money and being strict with her.

At 11, her mother and stepfather returned to Jamestown, and the couple brought the family back together. A year later, Ed encouraged Lucille to audition for a play put on by the local Shriners. They were looking for chorus girls for the production, and Lucille was cast. She loved the attention of the audience and wanted more. Being on stage was a way to get gratifying recognition.

Lucille Ball also enjoyed the attention of making others laugh, and she was always up for a dare. One such dare encouraged her to roller skate on the freshly varnished gymnasium floor. School administrators were unamused. Another incident found her speeding through the streets of Celoron, New York, outside of Jamestown, sitting on the front radiator of a boy's Tin Lizzy automobile. Her antics were not always comical. There were times when Lucille could be defiant—she often ran away from home and school. Occasionally, she left her classroom for a drink of water and never returned for the day. Instead, she spent the day doing other things. "Looking back," she wrote in her 1966 autobiography, *Love, Lucy*, "I think my main need was somebody to talk to, confide in—some wise and sympathetic older person." Her school principal Bernard Drake was that person. He labeled her antics "talent" and encouraged her to go on stage.

Many of the young people in Lucille's neighborhood got jobs in the amusement park next to her home. Lucille was hired as a short-order cook at the hamburger stand. She always thought of ways to attract customers and found success by abruptly hollering at passersby, "Look out! Look out! Don't step there." Startled and nervous about where their foot landed, the person stood stiff in their tracks, afraid to take another step. Lucille, then, continued with a lilt in her voice, "Step over here and get yourself a deee-licious hamburger."

At 12, her grandfather, Fred C. Hunt, lost everything—his family home, life savings, and personal belongings. It began when he accompanied Lucille, Fred, and Fred's friend Ruth to the backyard for target practice, carefully shooting the gun toward an open field with no nearby houses. Another young neighbor, eight-year-old Warren Erickson, came upon them. Realizing the boy had joined, her grandfather instructed him to "sit down and stay out of the way."

Sensitive to his mother's strict nature, Warren knew he must come running or suffer a spanking when his mother called for him. Just as Ruth took a shot, Warren's mother yelled his name. Instinctively, he got up and ran toward his house—passing in the line of fire. He was shot in the back and fell into lilac bushes. Though he survived the gunshot, he was paralyzed from the waist down—his spinal cord severed. Her grandfather was held responsible for the incident since the children were in his charge. At trial, one witness claimed that the man intentionally used the boy for target practice. Warren's mother also sued Lucille's grandfather, leaving the man penniless, and the incident ended with Lucille's intense dislike for guns.

At 14, it was apparent that Lucille was becoming a beauty. Her tomboy image was fading, and the boys took notice. She became infatuated with one such boy—23-year-old Johnny Devita. He was of Italian descent with a Mediterranean look about him. Johnny was studying to become a doctor until his mother needed him to go to work to support the family.

Lucille's mother strongly supported her desire to perform and encouraged her daughter to set out for New York to attend the John Murray Anderson School for Dramatic Arts. Her primary motivation was to put distance between Lucille and Johnny.

Soon after arriving, the school sent a letter home to her mother saying that Lucille was wasting her time and theirs. Lucille found the school intimidating and felt terrified. Yet, she became highly spellbound by the talents of her fellow students, especially the school's star pupil, Bette Davis. So, after only six weeks, she returned to Jamestown, periodically returning to New York with limited success on Broadway.

Two years later, at 16, she persuaded her mother to let her stay in New York to pursue an acting career. Lucille adopted the stage name, Diane Belmont. It had a ring of sophistication, and she always liked the name Diane. She adopted Belmont from the horse track.

Lucille found work as a model to pay the bills while pursuing her real passion—acting. Resuming the name Lucille Ball, the stunning brunette with big blue eyes dyed her hair blonde, as was the trend of the times. The hairstylist, Irma Kusely, believed that Lucille's personality was more suited to red hair, so she dyed it using the typical hair dye. But there was a problem getting the shade just right. Fortunately for Lucille, while performing in Las Vegas, she met a wealthy sheik who suggested she use henna to bring out the vibrant shade of red that became her signature look. He sent her a lifetime supply of henna, and the color it produced was so essential to Lucille's appearance that she kept the formula under lock and key.

One day, an artist friend painted a portrait of her sitting in an off-shoulder blue patterned dress, holding a cigarette between her fingers. He sold the painting to Chesterfield brand cigarettes. The company immediately hired Lucille as its "Chesterfield Cigarette Girl," and she quickly received national exposure. Her face, displayed on billboards throughout the country, opened new opportunities. She was offered a replacement role for one of the Goldwyn Girls in the Eddie Cantor musical comedy film *Roman Scandals* (1933) and moved to Hollywood, California.

Lucille, then 29, starred in the RKO Radio Pictures' film *Too Many Girls* opposite Cuban bandleader and bongo player from Santiago de Cuba, Desiderio Alberto Arnaz y de Acha III, also known as Desi Arnaz. Though he was six years younger, Lucy fell in love at first sight. The relationship progressed quickly, and in 1940, using a cheap wedding band from Woolworths, the two eloped to Greenwich, Connecticut. After the wedding, Desi continued to tour with his band, and Lucy made movies.

In 1950, Lucy was performing on a radio program titled *My Favorite Husband* when CBS approached her about adapting it into a live television program. Once Lucy insisted her husband, Desi, play her on-screen husband, CBS reneged. In turn, the couple developed their own production company—Desilu Productions. The couple took the show's concept on the road to prove that American audiences would, indeed, accept intercultural marriages. Audiences loved the act, and CBS executives admitted their error in judgment. The network agreed to produce the show.

Lucille enjoyed performing before a live studio audience, so CBS agreed to a live audience sound stage, along with the show's filming. For the first time in television history, a program was filmed for syndicated reruns using kinescopes—a multi-film camera setup using adjacent sets in front of a live audience. Desi Arnaz and cameraman Karl Freund developed the kinescope. Though the technique created additional production costs, Desilu agreed to pay the overage. The filming process became the industry standard production method for situation comedies. In addition, Desilu owned and controlled all rights to the film prints and the negatives, and it retained the revenue on all series reruns aired, making millions of dollars. It was a genius move. With their success, Desilu Productions produced shows such as *The Ann Sothern Show*, *The Untouchables*, *Star Trek*, *Mission Impossible*, and *The Sheriff of Cochise*, to name a few.

On October 15, 1951, *I Love Lucy* was born, starring Lucille Ball, Desi Arnaz, William Frawley, and Vivian Vance. Their first born child, Lucie Desiree Arnaz, was born that same year. A year and a half later, the couple's son, Desi Arnaz Jr., was born, and *I Love Lucy* did not shy from the reality that Lucille was pregnant—they embraced it. Lucille's character, Lucy Ricardo, was having a baby, too.

In the Golden Age of television, saying "pregnant" was considered offensive. Instead, Lucy was "expecting." As Desi Arnaz's character Ricky Ricardo termed it in his deep Hispanic accent—"Lucy's 'spectin." On January 19, 1953, the episode titled *Lucy Goes to the Hospital* was choreographed so that the birth of their on-screen son and their real-life son Desi Jr. coincided while 44 million viewers tuned in—a record number until Elvis Presley debuted on the *Ed Sullivan Show* in 1956. Subsequently, Desiderio Alberto Arnaz IV (known professionally as Desi Arnaz Jr.) made the cover of the first-ever issue of *TV Guide* on April 3, 1953.

When production ended, and *I Love Lucy* went off the air, Desilu Productions bought RKO Studios, which produced hits such as *The Dick Van Dyke Show*, *The Andy Griffith Show*, and *My Three Sons*.

Throughout their marriage, tensions grew between the couple stemming from personality differences, the stress of working together, and continuous quarrels. After 20 years of marriage, Lucille filed for divorce, which became final on May 4, 1960.

In 1961, Lucille married comedian Gary Morton, and on March 2, 1963, Desi Arnaz married Edith Mack Hirsch. Having sold his portion of Desilu to Lucille, she became the first woman to own a major film studio. She continued to run Desilu, along with the help of her new husband, until she sold it in 1968 to Gulf+Western, later known as Paramount.

From 1962 to 1968, Lucille starred in her new television program, *The Lucy Show*, and in 1968, she created *Here's Lucy*, which ran until 1973. She relied on her old friend Vivian Vance as her costar in both programs.

Throughout the years, Desi Arnaz and Lucille Ball remained friends. He often said that "I Love Lucy" was not just a title to a show, and he proved it by sending her flowers on her birthday and their anniversary every year until his death. On December 2, 1986, at 69, Desi died of lung cancer. He was cremated, and his ashes were scattered at sea.

On April 17, 1989, Lucille Ball developed severe pains in her chest and underwent seven-hour open-heart surgery. She remained in the hospital for a short time and was sent home. Nine days later, on April 26, Lucille suffered a ruptured aorta and died. She was 77.

Lucille Ball and Desi Arnaz will always be remembered together through *I Love Lucy* reruns and the Lucy-Desi Museum, which is located in Jamestown, New York.

The term multifaceted is probably overused, but in the case of Lucille Ball, it may be an understatement. When I first launched into the TV and movie industry through founding my company, the Narrative Television Network, I got a crash course in what goes on both in front of and behind the camera. Anyone around the world who has watched television throughout the last half-century accepts Lucy as a fixture, and most of us have a favorite memorable scene.

Even though I haven't seen it for over forty years, I still vividly remember the mirror pantomime scene Lucille Ball did with Harpo Marx. People around the world are also familiar with the candy factory scene and the episode involving Lucy stomping grapes at a winery. She made everything seem easy, natural, and fun. Behind the camera, Lucy and Desi Arnaz literally changed the industry both in the way that they produced each episode as well as the way they syndicated their programming, which remains the standard today.

Lucy broke the mold, bucked the trends, and set the standard in everything she did, which is why she reminds us that she was never as worried about making mistakes as she was about not trying. Lucille Ball left a legacy of creativity, success, and laughter.

9

*"Power is like being a lady...if you have to
tell people you are, you aren't."*

MARGARET THATCHER

MARGARET HILDA ROBERTS THATCHER, known as the esteemed
Baroness Thatcher of Kesteven upon being bestowed a life peer-
age honor—a distinction that entitled her to sit in the House of
Lords—was born on October 13, 1925, in Grantham Lincolnshire,
England. She became the longest, continuously serving British
Prime Minister of Great Britain and Northern Ireland since Robert
Jenkinson, 2nd Earl of Liverpool, and Robert Gascoyne-Cecil, 3rd
Marquess of Salisbury, in the 1800s. She was elected Leader of the
Conservative Party from 1975 to 1990 and won three consecutive
terms as Prime Minister, reigning from 1979 to 1990. To her credit,
she was the first woman to hold the office of Prime Minister in the
United Kingdom, making her husband, Sir Denis Thatcher, the first
male prime ministerial spouse.

During her tenure as a member of parliament, Margaret Thatcher
accelerated the growth of the British economy and became the
United Kingdom's most renowned political leader since Winston
Churchill. Under her leadership, she implemented policies known

as "Thatcherism," chiefly comprised of monetarism, privatization of industry, and labor union reform. Her tough, steely, and uncompromising leadership style earned her the moniker "Iron Lady," as one Soviet Union press journalist wrote, for her stance on Communism.

One of Margaret Thatcher's most defining characteristics, aside from her cobalt blue power suits, boxy handbag, and flawlessly molded hairstyle, was the distinctive articulation of her words. Every nuance of her image was consciously considered. She spoke slowly and precisely, and it is said that it was due to receiving elocution lessons early in her career to project a more commanding voice.

Her father, Alfred Roberts, was a tobacconist, grocer, Methodist preacher, and local alderman—a high-ranking crown official. Later, he became the mayor of Grantham. Under his influence, Margaret showed interest in politics and world events from an early age. When she was a young girl, the Roberts family gave refuge to a young Jewish girl escaping Nazi Germany during World War II. Margaret and her older sister, Muriel, used their savings to pay for the girl's journey to England.

Aside from her political aspirations, Margaret Thatcher's interests growing up included piano, field hockey, poetry recitals, and swimming. In her spare time, she volunteered as a fire watcher for the local Air Raid Protection (ARP) service and was assigned to a lookout tower to spot smoke caused by wildfires.

Margaret Roberts's intellectual aptitude afforded her a scholarship to study chemistry at Somerville College, Oxford, where she became active in its political arena and served as president of the college's conservative associations. She graduated in 1947 with a second-class degree in chemistry, specializing in X-ray crystallography—an experimental science that determines the atomic and molecular structure of crystals—and worked for the next four years as a research chemist. All the while, she studied for the bar examination in her spare time.

As a food scientist, she found employment at J. Lyons and Co., a well-known British restaurant chain, food manufacturing, and hotel conglomerate, and her team developed additives for ice cream. It is said that the company partnered with an American ice cream truck franchisor, Mister Softee, Inc., eventually discovering the "soft serve" variety of products simply by doubling the air in ice cream during the freezing process.

In February 1949, Margaret Roberts, then a chemist and recently selected parliamentary candidate, attended a Paint Trades Federation event in Dartford, England, where she met Denis Thatcher. Her first impression of him was tepid. She told her sister that he was "not a very attractive creature" and he was "very reserved but quite nice." In December 1951, they married.

Denis Thatcher was a wealthy industrialist and the managing director of his family-owned Atlas Preservatives, which employed 200 workers. Later, he became its chairman and led the paint and preservatives operation that expanded overseas.

By the early 1960s, Denis had gained sole control over the business. Though accounting and the stock exchange were the cornerstones of his training, he was a poor investor, and by 1965 the stress of running the entire family operation impacted his mental well-being. He sold Atlas Preservatives to Castrol for a significant price (£530,000 or £10,491,000 in today's UK economy) but remained managing director. This windfall afforded him the luxury of purchasing homes for his family in Chelsea, London, and Lamberhurst, Kent. Unfortunately, his poor financial management left only a seemingly moderate legacy by the end of his life.

In 1953, two years into their marriage, Margaret Thatcher gave birth, seven weeks prematurely, to twins—a son, Mark, and a daughter, Carol. Her husband welcomed her political ambitions and supported Margaret's entry into politics by financing her education as a barrister. The same year, she met the Bar Association requirements and began specializing in tax laws.

Margaret Thatcher moved up the ranks through the years using her political talents and ambitious nature. Early in her twenties, some predicted she would become Prime Minister one day. However, pessimistically, she stated as late as 1970, "There will not be a woman Prime Minister in my lifetime—the male population is too prejudiced." Nonetheless, she was elected Prime Minister in 1979. Margaret's political career had many highs and lows. Though she was revered for her swift victory in the 74-day Falklands War in 1982—when Argentina invaded the Falkland Islands—her popularity plummeted due to her economic policies.

One of her lows included abolishing free milk for school children aged seven to eleven when forced to reduce expenditures in the state education system. This action prompted the media headline "Margaret Thatcher, Milk Snatcher." In the wake of the event, she considered leaving politics. In her autobiography, she recalled the experience saying, "I learned a valuable lesson [from the experience]. I had incurred the maximum of political odium [hatred] for the minimum of political benefit."

Perhaps her tax law background led her to the theory that to ensure all citizens pay their fair share of government taxes, a Community Tax, more commonly known as the Poll Tax, would be a viable solution to improve the country's economic status. The tax levied changed from payments based on property values to a fixed amount per adult person in the household, regardless of income. Taxpayers earning lower incomes deemed it unfair and burdensome, especially those households with multiple family members. It was not so crushing for the more influential individuals earning higher incomes. The Poll Tax was often linked to the people's right to vote.

The tax assessment, imposed in Scotland in 1989 and England and Wales in 1990, met with public disobedience, mass protests, and rioting in the streets. The raging public anger resulted in individuals refusing to pay the tax, legal battles, and failure to report household members, which reduced the constituency at the voting polls.

In November 1990, Margaret Thatcher's leadership was challenged by Michael Heseltine for Conservative Leadership in the election. Each of the three opposition candidates vowed to rescind the Poll Tax should he be elected. By a narrow margin of 50 votes, Margaret prevailed in the first-round election but decided that rather than fail to win in the second-round ballot, she would resign. Her resignation came on November 22, 1990, ending her 15-year career as Conservative leader and 11-year reign as Prime Minister. Ultimately, Heseltine lost to John Major on the second ballot. The poll tax was abolished on March 21, 1991.

In February 2007, Margaret Thatcher became the first living British Prime Minister to have a bronze statue erected in the House of Parliament. It stands opposite to that of Winston Churchill's tribute.

On April 8, 2013, nearly ten years after losing her husband to inoperable pancreatic cancer, Margaret Thatcher died at her home at the elegant Ritz London, a 5-star hotel on Piccadilly in Mayfair. The United Kingdom began planning her funeral in 2009 by a committee chaired by Sir Malcolm Ross, former Master of the Royal Household. Per tradition, the committee gave the planning process a codename—*True Blue.* In all, the government spent a total cost of £3.6 million. She wished to receive a ceremonial funeral with full military honors at St. Paul's Cathedral rather than a state funeral.

Margaret Thatcher's death was marked with mixed emotions, from periods of high unemployment and social unrest to periods of great triumph. It has been reported that she was prouder of becoming the first Prime Minister with a science degree than being the first female Prime Minister.

Margaret Thatcher had one of the most important prerequisites to being a leader. She had a widely diverse educational and career background that gave her the ability to understand and relate to a wide variety of people and situations. While history has been kind to her and she will probably be even more greatly revered in the future, I believe she would be prouder of the respect and admiration of her peers than public opinion.

When speaking of world leaders, he admired or people he respected, US President Ronald Reagan invariably listed Margaret Thatcher among an elite handful of people he held in high esteem. I had the privilege of having a brief meeting with Mikhail Gorbachev shortly after the Berlin Wall came down, and the USSR crumbled. I remember asking him which world leaders he most respected and admired. Without hesitating, he said, "Margaret Thatcher stands alone."

She dominated the world stage during a turbulent time in history while she was breaking new ground for future generations of women. Her chapter-opening quote reminds us that both power and respect are earned from serving others, not taken from them.

10

"Give a girl the right shoes, and she can conquer the world."

MARILYN MONROE

NORMA JEANE MORTENSEN, known to her fans as Marilyn Monroe, was born on June 1, 1926, in Los Angeles, California. She began her career in the public spotlight as an iconic American pin-up girl and model after being discovered by photographer David Conover of the United States First Motion Picture Unit of the 18th Army Air Force Base while she was working in a factory during World War II. His mission was to shoot morale-boosting photographs of the female workers filling in for the deployed American male workforce.

Norma Jeane Mortensen's sex symbol image drew the attention of 20th Century Fox and Columbia Pictures, landing her short-term contracts for minor film roles in 1946. Fox executive Ben Lyon suggested that Norma Jeane change her first name to "Marilyn." The 1920s and 1930s Broadway actress and singer Marilyn Miller inspired the name. Taking her mother's maiden name, Norma Jeane forever became known as Marilyn Monroe.

After signing with 20th Century Fox, Monroe spent the next two years appearing in comedy film roles, including *As Young as You*

Feel and *Monkey Business*, and dramatic roles in *Clash by Night* and *Don't Bother to Knock*.

Marilyn Monroe first faced scandal when newspapers discovered that she once posed nude for a photographer before becoming a celebrity. Needing money to make a car payment, she posed under the name Mona Monroe for photographer Tom Kelley. She received $50 for the two-hour shoot. Several years later, Kelley sold the photos to Western Lithograph Company and converted them into a 1955 calendar titled "Golden Dreams." Ironically, the newspaper headlines only enhanced public interest in her films, and she became the top-billed actress for a decade.

The "blonde bombshell," as she was often characterized, became the leading sought-after Hollywood star by 1953. She landed leading roles in *Gentlemen Prefer Blondes*, *How to Marry a Millionaire*, and the crime drama film *Niagara*. All performances emphasized her sex appeal and established her image as a "dumb blonde." In all, Monroe appeared in at least 38 movies.

Her stardom and nude photographs earned her the cover and centerfold of the first-ever issue of *Playboy* magazine in December 1953. Hugh Hefner, the magazine's founder, never met Marilyn. Still, he purchased the rights to the photographs from the Chicago-based publishing company for $500 and featured them in his new and controversial magazine without her knowledge or consent.

In her words, "The magazine, I was told, thanks to my photos, [was] an instant sellout all across the country, an instant success," she reportedly told photographer George Barris, "I never even received a thank you from all those who made millions off a nude

Marilyn photograph. I even had to buy a copy of the magazine to see myself in it."

Marilyn Monroe's life was not always as alluring as it seemed to her fans. Early in her life, it was brimming with instability. In 1917, at 15, her mother, Gladys Pearl Monroe, married Jasper Newton Baker, nearly a decade her elder, and they had two children, Robert Kermit, known as Jackie, and Berniece Inez Gladys. Baker was an abusive man, and the couple divorced four years later. Although the court awarded Gladys custody, her ex-husband kidnapped their children and moved them to his home state of Kentucky. Monroe did not learn of her siblings until she was 12. By that time, 16-year-old Robert had died of renal failure due to tuberculosis of the bone.

Gladys Baker remarried Norwegian immigrant Martin Edward Mortensen in 1924.

While working as a film cutter for Consolidated Film Industries, Gladys met Charles Stanley Gifford and began a brief relationship. During their affair in 1925, she became pregnant with her third child, Norma Jeane. It was long presumed that Gifford was Monroe's biological father, and as an adult, she reached out to him. To her dismay, he rejected her claim of being his daughter and asked that she never contact him again. Gladys listed Norma Jeane's surname as Mortensen on her birth certificate at her mother, Della Monroe's, insistence to dispel illegitimacy allegations. Though the Mortensen couple divorced in 1928, two years after Norma Jean's birth in 1926, she was later baptized with Jasper Baker's surname.

In April 2022, nearly 60 years after Marilyn Monroe's death, French documentarian Francois Pomes had strands of her hair DNA tested—hair her embalmer had preserved, according to John

Reznikoff, president of University Archives in Connecticut. The results were the subject of Pomes's documentary, *Marilyn, Her Final Secret*. After comparing Monroe's DNA with the saliva sample provided by Gifford's great-granddaughter, Francine Gifford Deir, the results concluded, with 100 percent certainty, that Charles Stanley Gifford was Marilyn Monroe's biological father.

After Gladys divorced Mortensen, he was no longer in Monroe's life, and her mother could not emotionally or financially care for her. Monroe was traumatized to see her mother forcibly institutionalized, as she was plagued by mental illness. She spent most of her childhood living at the Los Angeles Orphans' Home and a total of 11 foster homes, suffering unspeakable abuses at nearly all. As a result, Monroe became shy and withdrawn, and she stuttered for a time. Finding relief from the woes of her environment, she spent most of her time attending movies—sitting in the front row, imagining life as a starlet.

In an attempt to free her from the foster system, in 1942 her mother encouraged her 16-year-old brunette beauty to marry the 21-year-old boy next door, James Dougherty. Dougherty was a factory worker who later became a Los Angeles police officer and the first trainer of the Special Weapons and Tactics group. He hardly knew Marilyn and was reluctant to wed a girl he considered "just a baby." However, Monroe dropped out of high school, and after a few weeks of getting to know each other, they married. For Monroe, it was an escape. The marriage hindered her career aspiration for stardom.

As her husband went off to serve in the Marine Corps in World War II, Norma Jeane chased a modeling career that landed her on the front page of hundreds of magazines. Her dream was coming true. According to her autobiography, *Marilyn Monroe: The Private Life of a Public Icon*, Dougherty would accept her modeling jobs if she quit when he returned from the Marines. When Dougherty returned in 1946, the couple divorced. She was unwilling to give up her dazzling lifestyle for the humdrum tasks of domestic life.

After being set up on a blind date with former baseball champion for the New York Yankees, Joe DiMaggio, Monroe fell in love with him. She later said that the sports star was "different" from other men. Rather than spending the evening bragging about his accomplishments to charm her, DiMaggio was reserved and soft-spoken. Monroe found those qualities endearing, and the next day, he sent her a large bouquet of roses.

The couple married in 1954, but in 1955, they divorced. Monroe allegedly claimed that DiMaggio was physically abusive and overly controlling. He presumed Monroe would quit her job and become a traditional housewife to him. He did not like that she was America's sex symbol and demanded she wear less-alluring clothing to minimalize her sex appeal. Ultimately, he realized Monroe would never give up her life of glitz and glamour in Hollywood. DiMaggio never stopped loving Monroe. Until the day he died, he sent roses to her grave every week, as she had once requested. It was reported by DiMaggio's attorney Morris Engelberg, that his last words before he died were, "I'll finally get to see Marilyn."

In 1956, Monroe married her long-time friend and playwright, Arthur Miller. He was best known for *A Death of a Salesman* and *After The Fall*, presumed to be written about Monroe and Miller's reflections on his failed marriage. Though she claimed at one point,

"This is the first time I've been really in love," in 1961, the two divorced when Monroe came across Miller's diary. He wrote an entry saying he was "embarrassed" by her. Arthur Miller supported his wife's ambitions to become a serious dramatic actor; but in the end, Monroe believed Miller used her notoriety to advance his career.

Scandal knocked on her door once more shortly before her death. On March 19, 1962, Marilyn Monroe performed a steamy and breathy rendition of "Happy Birthday" at President John F. Kennedy's 45th birthday celebration at Madison Square Garden dressed in a glamorous curve-hugging, flesh-colored sequined dress with more than 2,500 rhinestones beneath a white fur stole. When her stole was removed in a gesture symbolizing an unwrapped gift by President Kennedy's brother-in-law Peter Lawford, it appeared to the audience that she was wearing nothing but sparkle. From there, rumors circulated, romantically linking Monroe to the commander-in-chief. Perhaps no one will ever positively know the extent of their relationship for sure, but history makes presumptions. Though no resounding details are known relating to a torrid and persistent involvement with Kennedy, her legacy will forever link her to an affair—as it has for six decades.

Between 8:30 and 10:30 on the evening of August 4, 1962, Marilyn Monroe overdosed on barbiturates. Less than three months after her performance, in the early morning hours of August 5, her nude, lifeless body was discovered at her Brentwood home by her housekeeper. Deputy coroner Thomas Noguchi classified her death as a probable suicide. She was 36.

Marilyn Monroe was interred at Crypt No. 24 at the Corridor of Memories in Los Angeles at the Pierce Brothers Westwood Village

Memorial Park Cemetery. Her crypt is frequently blotted with lipstick kisses left by endearing fans.

Hugh Hefner, who never actually met Monroe, claimed he felt a kinship with the starlet. In 1992, he purchased the mausoleum drawer next to hers for $75,000, telling a newspaper reporter, "I'm a believer in things symbolic. Spending eternity next to Marilyn is too sweet to pass up." He died in 2017 and rests by her side.

Well beyond her death, Marilyn Monroe remains an iconic figure. In 1999, she was ranked sixth on the list of the greatest female screen legends from the Golden Age of Hollywood by the American Film Institute.

I will never forget the occasion when I was hired to speak for the top 500 producers for a national financial firm. They selected the Hollywood Wax Museum as the venue for their annual dinner and my speech. The corporation rented the entire wax museum and put a tent on the roof for the evening's program. The cocktail reception was held throughout the museum giving attendees the opportunity to have their photos taken with the various movie stars, athletes, political figures, and other celebrities.

I was intrigued by the fact that, among all of the individuals immortalized in the wax museum, the one figure more people were attracted to than any other was Marilyn Monroe. Obviously, she was a beautiful woman, but there were many other attractive women in the wax museum's displays. She was a movie star, but there were many far bigger stars and more renowned performers in the museum.

Marilyn had that certain intangible, indescribable element that can elevate someone to the greatest heights but can also be their downfall. It's important for us to put our best foot forward and make the best presentation we can both personally and professionally to the world. But we can never let our presentation or the image we offer become bigger than the essence of who we are and what we stand for.

11

"Bad taste is simply saying the truth before it should be said."

MEL BROOKS

MELVIN JAMES KAMINSKY, popularly known as Mel Brooks, became an actor, director, screenwriter, author, producer, composer, lyricist, filmmaker, and brilliant comedian with a flair for rhythmic-beat delivery that he credits to his passion as a drummer in his youth. Mel Brooks perfected the art of deliberate absurdity, nonsense, satire, and parody in his films like no other. From humble beginnings, he created a career spanning more than 70 years.

He was born of Jewish descent on June 28, 1926, in Brooklyn, New York. He grew up in the tenement neighborhood of Williamsburg with his beloved mother, Kate Brookman Kaminsky, and three older brothers, Irving, Lenny, and Bernie. After his father, Max, died of tuberculosis when Mel was two, Irving, ten years his senior, served as a surrogate dad to his brothers. Later, Mel passed the name Max to his character Maxwell Smart in the television show *Get Smart* and Max Bialystock in the film *The Producers*. He named his fourth child Maximillian "Max," who became an actor and best-selling author for his science fiction novel *World War Z: An Oral History of the Zombie War* (2006).

Despite his misfortune of living without a father, Mel had a terrific childhood as the youngest in the family. He recalls in his 2021 autobiography, *All About Me! My Remarkable Life in Show Business*, his brothers were wonderful: "We were like puppies in a cardboard box. We enjoyed one another's company tremendously—plenty of fights but plenty of fun."

In 1931, then five, Mel's brother Bernie took him to the Republic Movie Theatre to see *Frankenstein*, a film based on Mary Shelley's novel. To him, Frankenstein's monster was bigger than life, and it terrified him. That night, in the smoldering New York summer heat, before there was air conditioning, Mel insisted his bedroom window be kept tightly closed for fear that the monster would come through it, grab him by the neck, and eat him.

Insisting that the window be kept open for better air circulation, Mel's mother convinced him that such a notion was nonsense. She verbally traced the steps the creature would have to take to even get to the fifth floor at 365 South Third Street from Transylvania, Romania. She explained that to reach him, the creature would need to know transportation systems—boats, trains, buses, and ultimately the New York subways. Besides, she reasoned, he would come across the Rothstein family on the first floor long before even considering eating Mel on the fifth floor. By then, the monster's belly would probably be too full. Mel decided to take a chance and leave the window open. His mother always solved the many daily problems he handed her with patience and love. Ironically, later in life, Mel wrote the screenplay for *Young Frankenstein*, satirizing Dr. Frankenstein and his horrific creature.

Mel Brooks developed a talent for making people laugh as a kid. He was a petite young man and consistently found himself on the wrong side of bullying. Children can be cruel, and he became a popular target for their schoolyard dominance. He soon learned that comedy served as a viable weapon to protect himself. By making his enemies laugh, they became "frenemies."

In 1935, already a music lover at nine, Mel got his first Broadway musical fever. He was playing ball outside his tenement home when his cab driver uncle, Joe, came by and offered him a night at the theater. Uncle Joe had two free tickets to one of the biggest hits of the time, *Anything Goes*, at the Alvin Theater on West 52nd Street, later renamed the Neal Simon Theatre. He loved the excitement of the night; and after the show, Mel announced he was going into show business and that nothing would stop him. Nothing did.

At 14, Mel Kaminsky decided to become a drummer. He believed that his mother's maiden name, Brookman, was a more suitable stage name than Melvin Kaminsky, so he set out to paint Brookman on the front of his bass drum. After painting the letters B-R-O-O-K on the drum, there was no room for the remaining letters. Thus, he merely added one more—"S." He forever became known as Mel Brooks and legally changed his name.

Mel began his journey of making a name for himself by entertaining guests at the now-abandoned Borscht Belt Resorts in the Catskill Mountains. The Borscht Belt Resorts were popular, safe havens for vacationing Jewish New Yorkers, traditionally banned from most New York City hotels in the 1920s. Mel held the title "pool tummler" (entertainer), whose job was to amuse pool goers. One of his routines that made people laugh was pulling on a derby hat and alpaca coat and carrying two rock-filled suitcases. Approaching the pool, he stepped into it and sank to the bottom, setting off rolling laughter.

Brother Lenny was exceptionally good to Mel growing up. On Saturday nights, Lenny would flip Mel a half dollar, considered a small fortune in those days, and he used the money to go to the neighborhood Jewish delicatessen with his friends for a salami sandwich and a Dr. Brown's Cel-Ray Tonic—a celery-based soda. Then, he was off to a double feature at the local movie house. Afterward, with 15 cents remaining, he went to the ice cream parlor for a frappe—two scoops of vanilla ice cream smothered in chocolate syrup with a cherry on top. This routine fueled his lifelong love of movies.

In 1943, his mother had three blue stars hanging in her window. During World War II, the stars meant she had three boys serving their country. Soon, she would display four blue stars. Thankfully, the stars displayed were not gold, which announced that the family had lost a child in combat.

When he was 17 and in his senior year of high school in 1944, Mel figured it was inevitable that he would be drafted. So, he was on board when an Army recruiter came to his school to offer an admissions aptitude exam for entry into the Army Specialized Training Reserves program at the Virginia Military Institute. Passing the test entitled him to early graduation and government-funded college education. Officially, he was in the Army.

At 18, he trained in field artillery at Fort Sill, Oklahoma, specifically as a radio operator. Joining the troop transport for Normandy, France, on the liberty ship, the Sea Owl, he was both homesick and seasick. Once there, the Army determined he was better suited as a combat engineer. He learned to safely unearth landmines—trip wires attached to Shrapnellmines, also known as S-mines or Bouncing Betties. This device promised to maim rather than kill. His duties also included searching and clearing unsuspecting booby traps and building Bailey Bridges for troop convoys.

When the war ended, Mel remained in Germany as part of the Army of Occupation. His ability to sing, dance, tell jokes, and play the drums landed him a temporary invitation to join the special services unit. He became one of the comics in a variety show touring various Army camps.

Proving himself as a performer, Mel was transferred to special services and became a permanent entertainer for the troops. Life in the Army was suddenly not so daunting. Receiving recognition, Mel was featured in *Stars and Stripes*, the official military newspaper, with the headline, "A Star is Born." A year later, he was discharged, returned to the Borscht Belt hotels in the Catskills, and began a career as a stand-up comic, where he met fellow comedian Sid Caesar.

Mel broke into writing comedy through a brand-new medium— television. Soon, he landed a job on the writing staff of Sid Caesar's variety show, *Your Show of Shows*, which aired from 1950 to 1954. He went on to collaborate with other brilliant comedy writers to create memorable television programs and movies. Among the industry's classic comedy greats were Woody Allen, Neil Simon, Buck Henry, Larry Gelbart, best known as the creator of M*A*S*H, and Carl Reiner, who became his lifelong best friend until he died in 2020.

The duo Reiner and Brooks proved to be magic. Together, they created the comedy sketch *The 2,000-Year-Old Man*. In the adlibbed skits, Carl Reiner interviewed Mel Brooks, whose character was 2,000 years old. In one routine, Mel claimed to have witnessed the crucifixion of Jesus Christ, who, incidentally, "came in the store but never bought anything." In another, he shared that he had been married several hundred times, having "over forty-two thousand children, and not one comes to visit." The routine originated at house parties and was so hilarious that partygoers encouraged the pair to record an album.

From 1960 to 1997, they produced five albums. The first sold over a million copies. The success of their initial album led Mel Brooks to appear in the first-ever episode of *The Tonight Show*, starring Johnny Carson on October 1, 1962, along with Groucho Marks, Rudy Vallée, Joan Crawford, and Tony Bennett. Though the tape has since been lost, a voice recording of the program remains. Mel Brooks became a household name.

In 1961, Mel met actress and singer Anne Bancroft, best known as Mrs. Robinson in *The Graduate*, while watching her rehearse for her appearance on the *Perry Como Show*. Mel recounted in his book, "When the song was over, I leaped to my feet, applauded madly, and shouted, 'Anne Bancroft! I love you!'" It was "kismet," he said. "From that day until her death (2005), we were glued together."

Early in their relationship, Mel was reluctant to ask Anne to marry him until he found financial stability. After the success of the *2,000-Year-Old Man*, he finally proposed, and in 1964, they married at City Hall using one of Anne's hoop earrings as a wedding band because Mel forgot to purchase one. Together, they had one son,

Maximillian "Max," in 1972, extending his family of three children with his former wife, Florence Baum. The couple's marriage was full of laughter, and they were blissfully happy for 41 years. Anne used to say that when Mel came home, and she heard the key in the door, she knew "the party's about to start." Mel credits his success to Anne, saying she was "the guiding force" of his success. She encouraged his creativity in writing and developing the Broadway musicals *The Producers* (2001-2007) and *Young Frankenstein* (2007-2009).

Of all his creations, Mel Brooks is best known for writing, producing, and directing films. His famous works include the television comedy *Get Smart*, about a bumbling James Bond-inspired spy, and his movies such as *The Producers* (1967), *The Twelve Chairs* (1970), *Blazing Saddles* (1974), *Young Frankenstein* (1974), *Silent Movie* (1976), *High Anxiety* (1977), *History of the World, Part 1* (1981), *Spaceballs* (1987), and *Robin Hood: Men in Tights* (1993). In each of these films, Mel brought joy to his audiences and the cast and crews who brought his movies together. His persona made people laugh on and off-screen. Notably, his works made strong statements against racism, antisemitism, discrimination, and hostility toward Jews while making audiences laugh hysterically.

In 2006, *Blazing Saddles* was deemed "culturally, historically, and aesthetically significant" by the Library of Congress and was added to the National Film Registry for preservation. In 1974, it ranked as the second highest-grossing film in the US, whose underlying message addressed racial prejudice.

Having Mel Brooks's name associated with a film gave audiences the intuitive impression that the movie was a comedy. To separate his comedic films from the dramatic, he started his production company Brooksfilms in 1980, which solidified Mel Brooks's wide-range tastes and talent for drama. His first project was a movie Anne Bancroft wrote and directed called *Fatso*, starring Dom DeLuise. Under the company's banner, he also produced dramatic films, such as *The Elephant Man*, *Frances*, *The Fly*, *84 Charing Cross Roads*, and *My Favorite Year*.

As a tribute to a line in Mel Brooks's film *Blazing Saddles*, cofounders Michael DeSantis and Scotti Stark partnered in 2011 to bring a unique blend of red wine to Napa Valley—Harumph Wines. According to Mel, "I never got around to going as far as planting grapes and establishing a Mel Brooks vineyard. But funnily enough, a couple of guys who make wine up in Napa Valley named Scotti Stark and Michael DeSantis created a wine they dedicated to a signature phrase from *Blazing Saddles*. In the movie, when I make a speech as the governor, I expect a very big affirmative response from the audience, and when I don't get it, I angrily point to a man in the crowd and say, 'I didn't get a HARRUMPH out of that guy!' They seized on that word and, with my blessing, made a beautiful Cabernet Sauvignon called Harumph."

Mel Brooks won numerous awards for his creativity. He was the eighth person of 17 entertainers to earn an EGOT (Emmy, Grammy, Oscar, and Tony). During his 2015 appearance on *Real Time with Bill Maher*, Mel amusingly referred to himself as an EGOTAK. He created two additional letters by including the American Film Institute Award he received for three films he wrote and produced—*The Producers* (1967), *Blazing Saddles* (1974), and *Young Frankenstein* (1974), each ranked in the top 13 best cinematics on the American Film Institute's list of the top 100 comedies in the past 100 years—1900 to 2000, and his prestigious Kennedy Center Honor from 2009. Audiences of all ages continue to appreciate Mel Brooks's films, and scripted comedic lines from his movies are commonly requoted in everyday conversations worldwide.

In 2010, Mel Brooks received a Hollywood Walk of Fame star.

Among his many awards, in 2015, he received the National Medal of Arts, the highest honor the US government bestows. President Obama presented it "for his lifetime of making the world laugh."

People have asked Mel what inspired his comedic talents, thinking that it resulted from bitterness and anger over the loss of his father so early in life. On the contrary, he believes it is an extension of his wonderful childhood and his need to continue the magic of being a kid with his close-knit family. He loved entertaining them as a youth and enjoys making people laugh today. "I'm proud to say I have made people laugh for a living, and whether or not you'll allow me to, I'm going to brag—I can honestly say I've done it as well as anybody," Mel Brooks wrote in *All About Me!* "If you can laugh, you can get by. You can survive when things are bad if you have a sense of humor."

Mel Brooks possesses the sort of unparalleled genius that is easy to overlook at first glance. The absurd and farcical nature of his comedy can initially make it hard to take him seriously. In reality, the outrageous, over-the-top elements in a film like *Blazing Saddles*

actually lowers barriers and breaks through our cultural defense mechanisms so that Mr. Brooks can instruct us all on the insidious and destructive nature of racism.

I remember interviewing comic legend and the original host of *The Tonight Show*, Steve Allen, in the early 1990s. I asked if there were any subjects that were inappropriate or completely out of bounds for humor. Mr. Allen thought for several minutes, then said, "For mere mortals or regular human beings, I believe that the Holocaust should be avoided, but Mel Brooks is at another level." Healing begins when we can laugh at subjects as intense as our own mortality, racism, or even the Holocaust.

One of my treasured friends and movie producers often said, "If you can tell a great story, you earn the right to share your message." In his quote at the start of the chapter, Mel Brooks reminds us that if we can entertain people and make them laugh, we can earn the right to share some very powerful and relevant messages.

12

BASKETBALL HALL OF FAMER MICHAEL JEFFREY JORDAN, best known as MJ, burst on the sports scene as a professional basketball player for the Chicago Bulls in 1984. He was born on February 17, 1963, in the Fort Greene neighborhood in the northwestern section of New York City's Brooklyn borough to Deloris Peoples Jordan and James R. Jordan. Though he was born in New York, when MJ was young, his family moved to Wilmington, North Carolina.

In the 1980s and 1990s, MJ became a global cultural icon and popularized the sport of basketball. He was selected as the Chicago Bulls third overall pick in the NBA draft and signed a seven-year, $6 million deal. Standing 6' 6" tall, he played 15 seasons in the National Basketball Association, winning six NBA championships with the Bulls. Still today, his fans consider him the greatest basketball player of all time. He is well known for his incredible athleticism and uncanny ability to make every hoop shot look like a drop in the bucket.

Michael Jordan won a record ten scoring titles throughout his career, boasting a career average of 30.1 points per game, the most in NBA history, and a playoff record with an outstanding average of 33.45 points per game. The six-time NBA Champion was voted Most Valuable Player five times and won two Olympic gold medals as the United States men's national basketball team member in 1984 and 1992. He won four gold medals and one silver medal throughout his career tournament play.

The fourth of five children, MJ loved basketball and baseball at a young age. His brother Larry, standing only 5' 8" tall with a remarkable 44" vertical leap, was also a talented basketball player. After high school, Larry had high hopes of playing professionally. He played for the World Basketball League's Chicago Express in 1988. Perhaps the only thing standing in his way of a successful career like his brother's was his stature. As a child, Larry was the one person MJ often lost to during one-on-one challenges—until MJ hit a growth spurt. As Larry told ESPN, "I won most of them until he started to outgrow me, and then that was the end of that."

MJ's career jersey, number 23, became iconic and is a favorite among athletes of all sports. He explained his affinity for the number by saying, "My brother wore number 45, which was my number. So, when we were on the same team, we couldn't wear the same number. So, I chose half of what his jersey was, which was 22.5, which I would rather have 23." That is not to say that he did not have an opportunity to wear a different number. In 1990, he and his team were on the road and set to play against the Orlando Magic. Before the game, someone slipped into the locker room and stole his jersey. He was forced to wear a nameless jersey with the number 12 displayed on the back. Incensed by the incident, MJ managed to score 49 points in that game, proving he played well under emotional pressure.

Off-court, MJ is an American businessman. He is the principal owner and chairman of the Charlotte Hornets basketball team in North Carolina. He also owns an interest in DraftKings, a daily fantasy sports contest and sports betting company. In 2021, he partnered with 2020 Daytona 500 winner Denny Hamlin of the NASCAR Cup Series racing team, 23XI (pronounced twenty-three eleven) Racing, which bears his iconic jersey number 23.

Having a passion for golf, in 2019, he opened a prestigious course, The Grove XXIII Golf Club, near Hobe Sound, Florida, with 100 invitation-only members.

Michael Jordan's entrepreneurial talents exceed his athletic interests, and his business ventures are varied. Since his final retirement from basketball in 2003, he has built a lucrative career and uses his wealth for charitable and philanthropic purposes. Among them are the Boys and Girls Clubs of America, United Negro College Fund, Special Olympics, and other foundations.

In 1998, he opened an MJ Steak House restaurant with locations in New York City and Illinois and an MJ23 Sports Café in Connecticut. His restaurants serve Michael Jordan's own Cincoro Tequila, a brand he owns with five NBA team owners. Within his Chicago location, he has a table exclusively reserved for his dining experience—Table 23. Guests are welcome to book the table for a pre-set menu at a pre-fixed price. However, when Michael Jordan enters the restaurant, the waiter must relocate the party to another table to finish the meal. The good news—if that happens, the price of the meal becomes complimentary to the diners.

Among his endeavors, he owns the Michael Jordan Nissan car dealership in Durham, North Carolina. In the early days of his career, before purchasing a dealership, he took a trip to a car lot and bought seven vehicles in a single day. All except one was set aside for his family—a 1996 deep navy-blue metallic Mercedes-Benz W140 S600 coupe.

In addition to his basketball and NASCAR business ventures, MJ earns an astonishing sum annually from his "Air Jordan" athletic line of shoes, partnering with the American athletic-wear company Nike, a name inspired by the Greek goddess of victory.

Early in his career, while other athletic shoe companies, such as Adidas and Converse, wooed MJ with attractive endorsement deals, Nike offered him a percentage of the brand and an all-new, tailored-made shoe. It accommodated his specific need—shoes lower to the ground, each foot in a different size to meet his left being size 13 and his right 13.5. Accepting the Nike deal, in the first two months on the market, Nike sold $70 million worth of "Air Jordan" sneakers. Since the first "Air Jordan 1" debuted in April 1985, there have been 35 editions. Today, he continues to earn more in endorsements than any NBA star.

Based on his Nike deal, on October 18, 1984, in the preseason game against the New York Knicks, MJ pushed the league rule boundaries by wearing the unique black and red Nike sneakers. It was in a time when players primarily wore white athletic shoes with one corresponding team jersey accent color. NBA commissioner David Stern opposed "the wearing of certain red and black Nike basketball shoes" and not adhering to the league's "uniformity of uniform" rule, wherein players were prohibited from wearing shoes that did not match the team's uniforms or their teammates' shoes. According to Drew Hammell of @Nikestories, MJ was fined $5,000 each time he wore non-color-code-compliant sneakers on the court, and each time, Nike picked up the cost of the penalty.

The iconic Jumpman logo, a jump shot silhouette of Michael Jordan owned by Nike to promote the Air Jordan basketball sneakers, has become one of the world's most recognized brands. First introduced during a photo shoot for *Life* magazine shortly before the 1984 Olympic Games, it represents the zeal, dream, and achievements of Michael Jordan.

Soon after MJ won his third NBA title with the Bulls in 1993, his father and close friend, James R. Jordan Sr., was randomly murdered. A fisherman discovered his decomposed body in Gum Swamp Creek in South Carolina 11 days later. Sixty miles away, near Fayetteville, North Carolina, authorities found his Lexus SC400 sports car with its windows broken. There was evidence someone ransacked it.

As the story goes, on July 23, 1993, 18-year-old former classmates Daniel Green and Larry Demery decided to rob a motel. But when they came across James Jordan sleeping in his car, they decided to rob him. When Jordan woke, they shot him in the chest and drove his body to the creek. They rifled through his car and realized his identity. Demery testified at trial that he said to Green, "I believe we've killed Michael Jordan's daddy." Later, they used the stolen car to pick up their dates.

Days afterward, the two appeared in a home rap music video. Demery was wearing Michael Jordan's Nike Air golf shoes, and Green flashed the 1986 NBA All-Star ring MJ gave his father. With numerous tips from the public, the two were arrested and charged with the killing. They were sentenced to life in prison, serving in two separate North Carolina penitentiaries. Green has maintained his innocence, while Demery pled guilty to first-degree murder, armed robbery, and conspiracy to commit robbery.

MJ was devastated by the senseless loss of his father. The stress it caused, and perhaps gambling accusations, prompted the basketball star to lose his zest for the game. In a press conference on October 6, 1993, he announced his decision to retire after nine years. He said, "At this particular time in my career, I've reached the pinnacle of my career. I've achieved a lot in a short amount of time if you want to call it short, but I just feel I don't have anything for myself to prove." In speaking of his father, he said, "My father, as everyone knows, left us...I guess the biggest positive thing I can take out of my father not being here with me today is that he saw my last basketball game, and that means a lot."

Following his retirement, in the 1994 and 1995 baseball seasons, MJ changed careers by playing for the Chicago White Sox minor league baseball team, the Birmingham Barons. His 17-month experience on the team proved his strong work ethic. He practiced five days a week—before breakfast, pre-game batting, and post-game practice. After the games, he stayed long past his teammates, honing his skills. His career stats were not stellar during his stint in baseball, with 88 hits, 17 doubles, one triple, three homers, 51 runs batted in, and 46 runs scored.

On August 12, 1994, Major League Baseball was beset by a dispute between the owners and the players that led to a 232-day strike. MJ refused to cross the picket line as a replacement player and returned to basketball. Had there not been a baseball strike, it may have forever changed his career path.

For the 1994-1995 regular season play, he returned to the Chicago Bulls only to retire a second time on January 13, 1999, believing it was time. But that was not the end of his basketball career. MJ, once again, returned to basketball in 2001, playing with the Washington Wizards. In the wake of the September 11 assault on the United States, he donated his first year's salary to its relief efforts—$900,000 divided among various charitable organizations and $100,000 to the children who lost parents in the tragic attack. Michael Jordan's time with the team lasted for two seasons before calling it quits for the third time in 2003.

To date, there has never been a player who has risen to the challenges of basketball more than Michael Jordan. In June 2010, *Forbes* ranked him the 20th most powerful celebrity in the world, and in 2014, he became the first NBA player to rise to billionaire status.

Michael Jordan has proven his place in basketball and earned a place in history.

When we consider Michael Jordan's quote cited at the beginning of this chapter, it is readily apparent relating to basketball and business, he wanted it, wished it, and made it happen at a level few, if any, have equaled.

Michael Jordan remains the embodiment of excellence to people around the world. In one of the most competitive areas of life, he has proven to stand out even among all-stars and hall-of-famers.

Beyond his commitment, effort, and success, Michael Jordan will always remind me of the need to focus and maximize our talent.

While he was one of the greatest athletes in the world while playing basketball, Michael Jordan's best efforts only resulted in him becoming a mediocre Minor League baseball player. If he had decided to pursue baseball throughout his entire career, you and I would have never heard of Michael Jordan.

Success in life is a matter of finding our talents and gifts and then bringing them to the world in a way that serves others.

13

"That's one small step for man, one giant leap for mankind."

NEIL ARMSTRONG

NEIL ALDEN ARMSTRONG, born on August 5, 1930, fulfilled his dreams by becoming an American naval aviator, test pilot, astronaut, and aeronautical engineer. After retiring from NASA in August 1971, he became a university professor in the Aerospace Engineering department at the University of Cincinnati. After eight years of teaching, he resigned and left the university.

Neil Armstrong came into this world on his family's 187-acre farm outside of Wapakoneta, Ohio, to Stephen Armstrong, an auditor for the state of Ohio, and Viola Engel Armstrong. He had a younger sister, June, and a younger brother, Dean. His father's job moved the family around the state for the next 14 years, eventually settling back in Wapakoneta.

Armstrong was a quiet child but made an impressive impact on teachers with his perfect-score tests. As a boy, his ability to build model airplanes fascinated others. He displayed the replicas by hanging them from his bedroom ceiling. For fear of damage during flight or when landing, he did not fly them. Perhaps this led to his reoccurring dream of hovering above the Earth like an airplane merely by holding his breath.

One day, at age six, Armstrong and his father were on their way to church. They saw an airfield and stopped to explore. For a couple of dimes, the pilot of a monoplane, known as a "Tin Goose," offered them a ride high above the Earth. Knowing his son's fascination with model airplanes, he knew it would excite him. The experience significantly impacted Armstrong—he decided then to be a pilot.

Armstrong worked at Rhine and Brading Drug Store through high school to earn extra money. His wage was 40 cents an hour, and he worked 23 hours weekly. When he had saved $9, enough money for a flying lesson, he asked for time off from the drug store, hopped on his bicycle, and peddled to the airfield just a few miles away. The landing strip was constructed among the corn, hay, and bean fields. Armstrong was merely a passenger starting out but progressed to operating the aircraft. On his sixteenth birthday, he had earned enough instructional hours to get his pilot's license—even before he had a driver's license.

In his hometown lived a man people called the "Wizard of Wapakoneta." An engineer at Westinghouse, his name was Jacob Zint. The man lived in a brick home with an observatory built on top of his garage with a domed rotunda that turned on roller skate wheels. He invited his neighbors, by appointment only, to climb the stairs to view the moon and the stars. All were thousands of miles away yet seemed within reach through his telescope.

One night in 1946, 16-year-old Armstrong, nearing his distinguished Eagle Scout badge—the highest rank attainable in the Boy Scouts of America organization—needed his Astronomy Merit

Badge. With a reservation, of course, Troop 14 visited the observatory on the path to answer three essential questions to earn their patch: Why is a year 365 days? Why is a day 24 hours? Why does the Earth have seasons? Together, the troop identified constellations and got a sense of their place in the universe. That was the night Neil Armstrong connected with the moon, the stars, and the Earth's travel through space.

Attending college at 17, he was accepted to Purdue University in West Lafayette, Indiana, and the Massachusetts Institute of Technology (MIT). Armstrong opted for Purdue to study aeronautical engineering over the longer distance travel from his home in Ohio to Cambridge, Massachusetts. His tuition was paid for under the Holloway Plan, a program enacted by Harry S. Truman in 1946. It was designed by Admiral James Holloway Jr., USN Chief of the Bureau of Personnel, to ensure adequate Navy Flight Training personnel between wars. Under the plan, known as "AN ACT," individuals who desired to fly had to commit to two years of study at a university, followed by two years of flight training and one year of service as an aviator in the US Navy. After military service, candidates returned to the university to complete their final two years of study and receive a bachelor's degree.

In September 1951, Armstrong, serving as an escort for a photo reconnaissance mission over Songjin, Korea, flew an F9F Panther over the country's primary transportation and storage facility. There, he had a life-threatening experience. While flying a low-bombing run at 350 miles per hour, his plane flew into a cable strung across the hills intended as a booby trap to disable low-flying enemy aircraft. Amid the heavy artillery fire in the area, the wire tore off two feet of a wing when it collided. Attempting to recover, Armstrong flew toward the ocean, away from the enemy territory, but was forced to eject. Despite his efforts, the wind drug his parachute, landing him back into enemy territory. With luck on his side, an American military vehicle soon rolled by and picked him up. Pleasantly surprised, he discovered the driver was a friend from flight school.

While attending Purdue University, Armstrong met his first wife, Janet, at an Alpha Chi Omega party. She had been studying home economics. They married in 1956 and moved to California, where Armstrong became a test pilot at Edwards Air Force Base near Lancaster. When the opportunity arose on flights over their home, he tipped the plane's wings to say "hello" to his wife and his first son, Rick.

The couple had two more children—Karen Anne and Mark. Their second child, Karen Anne, who he affectionately called "Muffie," died on January 28, 1962, at only two and a half years old. Ultimately, she died of pneumonia—a complication resulting from a highly aggressive and difficult-to-treat brain stem tumor known as Diffuse Intrinsic Pontine Glioma (DIPG). Her death fell on her parents' sixth wedding anniversary.

Devastated by Karen's death, Armstrong and his family soon decided to leave California and move to Houston, Texas. Armstrong was selected for a new project with the National Aeronautics and Space Administration's (NASA) Astronaut Corps. Though not considered their top performer, he flew his first mission in 1965 as a backup crew member. A year later, he became Commander of the Gemini VIII flight, which ran into trouble when the orbital flight attitude control thrusters fired suddenly and spun out of control.

Had Armstrong not kept his composure, accurately diagnosed the problem, and taken corrective action, both astronauts on board would have perished. During the mishap, he and his pilot David Scott experienced vertigo and the physiological effects of the acceleration tumbling and the spacecraft's plummeting.

Although he controlled the flight, the crew was forced to eject for a landing 100 feet above the Earth. The Gemini crew could have been lost if not for coolheaded Armstrong. An hour later, he was seen diligently completing the post-flight paperwork in his office as though nothing had happened. When asked how he could be so calm after an incident of such magnitude, he said, "There was work to be done."

In November 1967, he was selected as Commander of the Apollo 11 Lunar Mission and became the first person to step out of the module and onto the moon's surface. The White House wanted the mission commander to be a civilian and chose Armstrong for his likable personality, quiet confidence, and calmness. He never took shortcuts or panicked under pressure. Going beyond his aspirations, at 38, with his depth of experience and nerves of steel, "Astronaut" became his third job title after Navy Pilot and Research Test Pilot.

On July 20, 1969, the United States fulfilled President John F. Kennedy's dream "of landing a man on the moon and returning him safely to the Earth" and winning the Space Race with the Soviet Union before the end of that decade—a dream realized six years after his death.

Addressing a large crowd gathered at Rice University in Houston, Texas, on September 12, 1962, Kennedy declared, "We choose to go to the moon in this decade and do the other things, not because they are easy, because they are hard...." With an estimated 650 million viewers worldwide watching the blurry images of the historical landing on their television sets, the Apollo 11 Lunar Module, launched from the Kennedy Space Center four days prior, transporting its three-person crew consisting of Commander Neil Armstrong, Lunar Module Pilot Edwin "Buzz" Aldrin, and Command Module Pilot Michael Collins.

Always a Boy Scout, Armstrong carried his World Scout Badge on his journey to the moon, and while in flight, he sent his regards to the attendees of the National Scout Jamboree in Idaho over the airwaves.

After traveling 240,000 miles in 76 hours, astronauts Armstrong and Aldrin moved from the Control Module Columbia to the Lunar Module Eagle, preparing for landing. It was apparent to the crew that the landing location would have put the craft awkwardly in a crater, making it impossible to lift off to return to Earth. With only 15 seconds of fuel left, Armstrong kept his composure, switched the control for a manual landing, and selected an alternative docking location.

At the same time, a panel alarm flashed the codes 1202 and 1201. Not even the programmer who designed the control knew what was happening. Computer programmer Don Eyles said, "The alarms were saying there's no more storage space. We're going to flush everything and sort of reconstruct it—do what you would call a restart." The event put dire panic into the pit of Eyles's stomach and a feeling that the mission was doomed.

Before aborting the mission, Mission Control realized that the computer was still running the critical guidance and navigation systems and made the courageous decision to proceed. Ultimately, the codes were traced to an obscure condition created by the radar accidentally being turned on. The computer became overloaded with unnecessary data. At the time, no one could identify the code—for 50 years, neither did much of the world. Fortunately, the codes were good, and the computer had explicitly done what it was supposed to do. The issue had been a human error—someone accidentally flipped a switch, limiting operation and speed.

The two-person crew landed on what they called "Tranquility Base." They docked on the southwestern corner of the dark lunar plain Mare Tranquillitatis, translated from Latin meaning "Sea of Tranquility." Upon touchdown, the world heard Armstrong say, "Houston, Tranquility Base here. The Eagle has landed." He was referring to the portion of the module that served as the craft's lunar lander, marked with a prominent bald eagle insignia.

After landing, Armstrong waited six hours and 39 minutes to step from the spacecraft. At 2:56, Coordinated Universal Time (known as UTC) on July 21, 1969, he described the surface as "Very, very fine-grained. As you get close to it, it's almost like a powder." Then, he uttered the famous words that live on in history, "That's one small step for man, one giant leap for mankind." Together with fellow astronaut Buzz Aldrin, who joined Armstrong 19 minutes later, they explored the moon for two hours.

According to journalist Jay Barbee's biography, Armstrong's daughter Karen never left his thoughts while moonwalking. Noticing a baby crater, he affectionately named it "Muffie's Crater."

Before departing, they planted a 3-by-5-foot American flag. Armstrong found the terrain challenging to penetrate, so he planted the flagpole no more than seven inches into the lunar surface. Unfortunately, images taken by NASA since that day show it no longer casts a shadow.

On his green desktop telephone, President Richard Nixon called the crew of Apollo 11 to congratulate them. He called it the longest-distance phone call ever made from the White House.

He said in his speech to the squad, "I just can't tell you how proud we all are of what you have done. For every American, this has to be the proudest day of our lives. And for people all over the world, I am sure that they, too, join with Americans in recognizing what an immense feat this is. Because of what you have done, the heavens have become a part of man's world, and as you talk to us from the Sea of Tranquility, it inspires us to re-double our efforts to bring peace and tranquility to Earth. For one priceless moment in the whole history of man, all the people on this Earth are truly one. One in their pride in which you have done and one in our prayers you will return safely to Earth."

On July 24, 1969, Armstrong, Aldrin, and Collins, who had remained in the Control Module, safely splashed down 900 miles off the coast of Hawaii. But before leaving the moon, Buzz Aldrin tossed a package out of the Lunar Module door. Inside was a patch with the names Edward White, Virgil "Gus" Grissom, and Roger Chaffee—astronauts who died on the launchpad at Cape Kennedy in a blazing fire during pre-launch testing of Apollo 1 on January 27, 1967. The package, authorized by NASA and known as a Personal Preference Kit (PPK), had to be small, limited in size and weight, and vacuumed packed. The package had been tucked away in Buzz Aldrin's shoulder pocket, and if not for Armstrong's reminder, it may never have been left behind on the moon's surface. As Aldrin was halfway up the lunar module ladder, Armstrong called, "How about that package out of your sleeve? Get that?" Aldrin pulled the packet out and tossed it onto the surface. Armstrong nudged it with his foot to brush the dust from it.

Armstrong never revealed the symbolic contents of his PPK mementos. However, it is believed to have contained an olive branch pin belonging to his wife, Janet, and an undisclosed item in memory of his daughter, Karen.

Also gifted to the moon was a silicon disc the size of a half-dollar etched with microscopic lettering—about one-fourth the width of a human hair. On it were messages of goodwill from 74 leaders worldwide. It included four presidential statements from the then-current US President, Richard M. Nixon, and past president Lyndon B. Johnson. There were quotes from the National Aeronautics and Space Act of 1958, signed by Dwight D. Eisenhower, John F. Kennedy's May 25, 1961, lunar landing commitment speech to Congress, and other historical references.

Later, in a post-flight press conference, Armstrong was asked about the mission and the spontaneity of his famous words spoken on landing. He said, "I always knew there was a good chance of being able to return to Earth, but I thought the chances of a successful touch down on the moon's surface were about even money—fifty-fifty. ...Most people don't realize how difficult the mission was. So, it didn't seem to me there was much point in thinking of something to say if we'd have to abort landing."

However, in 2012, his brother Dean revealed that Armstrong's chosen words were scripted months before the mission. He had sought advice on the quote while the two were playing a game of "Risk" before leaving for Cape Canaveral. Initially, he wrote, "That's one small step for *a* man, one giant leap for mankind," but omitted the word "a" as he spoke. Scripted or improvisation, it is a quote that lives on in history.

Upon his return from the mission, Armstrong addressed the US Congress. In his speech, he thanked them for the opportunity to witness some of the "grandest views of the Creator."

Neil Armstrong retired from NASA in 1970 and returned to Ohio. He bought a 125-year-old farmhouse surrounded by 200 acres of land in Lebanon, where he raised cattle and grew hay and beans. There, he took his sons to Boy Scout meetings, watched them play football, and attended 4-H auctions. He was frequently spotted at the Village Ice Cream Parlor, the Big Boy, and the gas station pump. But no one ever saw him at the air shows or parades thrown in his honor. His chats with the town's people merely included topics such as the weather, golf, or mowing.

After retirement, Armstrong completed his Master of Science in Aerospace Engineering degree and took a position as a professor at the University of Cincinnati, where he taught for eight years. He remained connected with NASA and participated in various commissions, including the Roger's Commission investigating the Space Shuttle Challenger explosion, which happened 73 seconds into its flight. The country mourned the lives of Commander Francis Scobee, Pilot Michael Smith, Judith Resnik, Ronald McNair, Ellison Onizuka, Gregory Jarvis, and the first civilian destined for space, teacher Christa McAuliffe.

Neil Armstrong never gave up his love of flying. He continued to fly his favorite plane—the glider—well into his 70s. He believed "real" flight was done in an aircraft without an engine. "It's all about managing energy. You are part of the equation," he told his college students. Before his moon flight, he had earned a gold badge with two diamonds from the International Gliding Commission. Eventually, he had to stop flying after developing a heart problem. In February 1991, he suffered a mild heart attack on a ski trip in Aspen, Colorado.

By 1990, Armstrong and his wife, Janet, separated and divorced in 1992 after 38 years of marriage. He later met Carol Held Knight at a golf tournament. They married on June 12, 1994, and moved to Indian Hill, Ohio. Through his relationship with Carol's daughter, Molly, he became father-in-law to the future New York Mets general manager Brodie Van Wagenen.

On April 6, 1985, a professional expedition leader, Mike Dunn, organized a North Pole expedition. He invited the "greatest explorers." The group included Neil Armstrong, Edmund Hillary, Hillary's son Peter, Steve Fossett, and Patrick Morrow. Armstrong once said that he was curious to see the North Pole from the ground, as he had only seen it from the moon.

Armstrong, and his fellow crew members, received the Presidential Medal of Freedom and the 1969 Collier Trophy. President Jimmy Carter presented him with the Congressional Space Medal of Honor in 1978, and in 1979, he was inducted into the National Aviation Hall of Fame. In 2009, Armstrong received the prestigious Congressional Gold Medal.

Neil Armstrong did not define himself as the first person to walk on the moon but by how he lived his life. When asked many times how it felt to be the first person to walk on the moon, he replied amusingly, "I got to go to more press conferences to answer the question: 'How did it feel to be the first person to walk on the moon.'" His family described him as a "reluctant American hero" who kept a low profile. Astronaut John Glenn told *CNN*, "[Armstrong] didn't feel that he should be huckstering himself. He was a humble person, and that's the way he remained after his lunar flight, as well as before."

In an interview in *The Cincinnati Enquirer* on July 19, 2009, Neil Armstrong summarized, "I like to think I am a relatively normal person who had some extraordinary experience." When asked what three words best described him, he responded, "very-lucky-fellow."

On August 7, 2012, Neil Armstrong entered Mercy Faith-Fairfield Hospital in Cincinnati to relieve his coronary artery disease. After developing complications from the bypass surgery, he died on August 25, at 82. He was buried at sea with military honors, and his ashes were pledged to the Atlantic Ocean. His personal papers and a staggering 70,000 pieces of fan mail were donated to Purdue University.

The following month, on September 13, a memorial service was held in his honor at the Washington National Cathedral in Washington, DC. Within the Cathedral is a Space Window that depicts the Apollo 11 mission. Amid the stained glass, the panel contains a sliver of moon rock. Among those who honored the life of Neil Armstrong at the ceremony were John Dalton, Former Navy Secretary, Former Command Module Pilot Michael Collins, and Retired Captain Eugene Cernan, Apollo 17 Commander and the last man to walk on the moon. Diana Krall appropriately sang, "Fly Me to the Moon."

NASA Administrator Charles Bolden, the former astronaut who flew on four Space Shuttle missions, once said, "As long as there are history books, Neil Armstrong will be included in them, remembered for taking humankind's first small step on a world beyond our own."

Despite his humble nature, Neil Armstrong was an American hero.

Throughout recorded history, the 20th century represents the greatest period of discovery, development, and innovation. If you had to take that amazing century and define it by one image, it would likely be Neil Armstrong walking on the moon. If you tried to put it into words, it would probably be best represented by Neil Armstrong's quote, "That's one small step for man, one giant leap for mankind."

Within that brief statement, Neil Armstrong pointed out that, while he was the person standing on the moon, he represented thousands of people who made it possible, millions of people watching him around the world, and several billion people on planet Earth who, for the first time, could consider the reality of human beings beyond our tiny blue planet.

As an 11-year-old, I remember watching Neil Armstrong climb down the ladder of the Eagle and step onto the surface of the moon.

Shortly after that momentous event, my mother and I went for a walk in our neighborhood. I was struck by the fact that there were no people outside of their homes and no traffic on the streets. As we passed each of the houses, I could hear the television broadcast emanating from every home. It was truly a worldwide event that brought us all together.

In addition to his immortal words as he stepped onto the moon, I will always remember Neil Armstrong through his quote that encompasses the massive undertaking and incredible endeavor that resulted in the success of the Apollo 11 mission. Neil Armstrong said, "Mystery creates wonder and wonder is the basis of man's desire to understand."

14

"I think more important than law is the hearts of people."

LOUIS GOSSETT JR.

LOUIS CAMERON GOSSETT JR. was born in Sheepshead Bay, Brooklyn, New York, on May 27, 1936, to Hellen Rebecca Wry Gossett, a nurse, and Louis Gossett Sr., a porter. He remains an American icon in the film and television industry with a career spanning seven decades. Since the early 1950s, Gossett has appeared in nearly 200 roles and delivered commanding performances alongside some of the biggest names in show business. He portrayed many characters, including a fighter pilot, a Marine drill instructor, a musician, a genie, and an alien, to name a few. His extraordinary acting talent landed him performances in *A Raisin in the Sun*, *The Landlord*, *Skin Game*, *Travels with My Aunt*, *The Laughing Policeman*, *The White Dawn*, *The Deep*, *Jaws 3-D*, *Enemy Mine*, *The Principal*, *Iron Eagle* movie series, *Toy Soldiers*, *The Punisher*, and *The Lamp*.

Gossett is best known for two outstanding performances. As Fiddler in Alex Haley's 1977 six-part mini-series *Roots*, he earned an Emmy Award. For his portrayal as Marine Gunnery Sergeant Emil Foley in the 1982 film *An Officer and a Gentleman*, he took home three distinguished awards—the Oscar, presented by the Academy

Awards for Best Supporting Actor, the Golden Globe Award for Best Supporting Actor—Motion Picture, and the NAACP Image Award for Outstanding Actor in a Motion Picture.

To prepare for the part of Emil Foley, Gossett spent 60 days in basic training at Camp Pendleton in San Diego, California. During his training, he ran obstacle courses, trained in hand-to-hand combat, developed skills in martial arts, and studied the life of a Marine drill instructor. Determined to deliver an authentic performance and remain true to his character, Gossett kept a distance between himself and the other actors on the set. His training and dedication to the authenticity of the role paid off, and winning the Oscar changed the quality of the acting roles he was offered.

According to Gossett, his most challenging role was portraying alien soldier Jareeba Sheegan in the 1985 science fiction *Enemy Mines*, filmed in Budapest and Munich. The part required six to seven hours of costume preparation each morning. He wore two tortuous contact lenses and heavy makeup that caused a painful skin rash. With the help of a first-year medical student, Gossett fully recovered.

Louis Gossett Jr. grew up in a diverse neighborhood in New York, surrounded by family and friends with various cultural backgrounds. One thing his close-knit community had in common was the people cared for one another. "At dinner, when I'd come home from school, I would take a deep breath, and I would smell my way around the world. I could smell fried chicken or corned beef and cabbage or menudo. It depended on who was home," he recalled.

The finest pastime among his friends was using their imaginations. On the playground, they magically transformed into television heroes, Western cowboys, and even Superman, but Gossett's childhood dream was to become a doctor—a brain surgeon and psychiatrist. The medical profession held a strong interest because many of his family members were not well—especially his grandmother's brother, who could not even stand, given his condition. But he also had a passion for basketball. Standing 6' 4", he showed exceptional talent for the sport and hoped to become a professional player one day.

Gossett served as class president and captain of the basketball and baseball teams in school. After suffering a sports injury, he could not play on the team. At age 17, his life suddenly veered in another direction, and he passed his rehabilitation time by enrolling in an acting class. He appeared in the school play, *You Can't Take It with You*, and when it ended, he returned to basketball for the season.

As a senior at Abraham Lincoln High School, Gossett's English teacher, Gustaf Bloomburg, whom they called Gus Bloom, saw his talent and ability to bring his stage character to life. Bloom knew that playwright Louis Peterson was producing the full-length play, *Take a Giant Step* on Broadway at the Lyceum Theater and said to Gossett, "Louis, they're looking for a young black kid about your age. They went through all the high schools and can't find anybody. Tell your mother to take you down there on Sunday. What can you lose?"

That Sunday, he went to the theatre and auditioned for the starring role of Spencer. He was interrupted during the audition when Peterson began giggling at him. Embarrassed, Gossett turned from the stage and left. Fortunately, Peterson caught up with him and said, "We weren't laughing at you. You remind me of myself when I was your age. Come back." Convinced, Gossett continued the audition and got the part. The only condition to getting the role was that he worked hard to mask his Brooklyn Jewish accent.

His grandmother, Bertha Wry, began her life as an enslaved person from Georgia and lived to be 115 years old. She never attended school or learned to count, but she inspired Louis Gossett Jr. In 1953, she was poised in the audience during one of his performances as Spencer in *Take a Giant Step*. In the play, there was one line of dialogue in which Gossett's character said, "Dammit, Grandma, I'm not going to do that." After the show, he was backstage with artists such as Duke Ellington, Count Basie, and other cast members. Bertha found her way backstage, and suddenly he heard, "Get outta the way." Everybody obeyed as she pushed through the crowd.

Happy to see her, Gossett shouted, "Grandma!"

As she approached him, she slapped him in the face.

"Grandma, what are you doing?" he asked, and she slapped him again.

"You sass your grandma one more time...I taught you better than that."

"But Grandma, that's the line in the play."

As she walked out, she said, "I don't care, and tomorrow I'm coming back to make sure you don't do it again."

Gossett stood stunned and embarrassed while everyone laughed.

As Gossett recalled of his grandmother, "She only lied to me one time—when she said, 'This is going to hurt me more than it hurts you.'"

Take a Giant Step ran for eight weeks, and for his performance he earned The Donaldson Award for Best Newcomer.

Upon leaving high school, Gossett was offered an athletic scholarship but turned it down. Instead, he enrolled in medical school—at Bellville in Chicago. Gossett was a good student until one day he dissected a cat's brain, its leg involuntarily lifted, and it was on to drama school instead.

At 23, Louis Gossett Jr. worked with Broadway legends such as Sydney Portier, Ruby Dee, and Maxine Sullivan in the Broadway production of *A Raisin in the Sun*. As an original cast member, he played George Murchison, a wealthy, well-educated man with academic achievements. His fellow actors taught him the art of acting, and he fell in love with the craft.

In 1959, Gossett was invited to the rookie camp in the Catskills of New York—drafted to play for the Knickerbockers. The team's name was initially drawn from a hat and referred to the style of trousers Dutch settlers wore in 1625. Today they are called the Knicks. Though he had just signed with *A Raisin in the Sun* production, he was curious to see if he could make it professionally. Soon he realized that, in those days, he had more money in his pocket by acting than the basketball team had in the bank. He also discovered there was a lot of violence among the young men. Fist fights and feuds broke out among the players regularly. Choosing acting over violence, he stepped away from his dream of professional sports and committed to performing full-time.

Louis Gossett Jr. married three times. In 1967, he married Hattie Glascoe, but the marriage lasted only one year and was annulled. Gossett married his second wife, Christina Mangosing, in 1973, and they welcomed a son, Satie. Sadly, that marriage ended in 1975. His third marriage was to *Star Search* champion Cyndi James-Reese in 1987. Together, they adopted a boy.

One day in 1986, a television field report caught his attention while watching *Good Morning America's* news program. The story recapped the plight of hungry and homeless children in America. In the interview, the reporter talked with Sharron Anthony, a 9-year-old African-American boy from St. Louis, Missouri. The reporter asked, "If you had one wish, what would it be?" The boy replied, "For something to eat and a place to stay." The touching story pulled Gossett's heartstrings and led him to contact the network to find the boy who needed a good home. Before long, the couple adopted Sharron. Reflecting on his decision, Gossett said, "I had an Oscar, and I had an Emmy. I had all the trappings of success. My heart is fuller now that I have that young boy. Now I have my family."

Along his journey, Gossett fell victim to fame and fortune, making some questionable choices, he admits, spending time partying and attending nightclubs. Fortunately, he put his life back on track and recommitted to his craft. His career has taken him to many places and given him exceptional opportunities to learn about people of cultures and make life-long friends. He has lived in Israel, England, Mexico City, Iceland, and Egypt.

With a passion for peace and dignity among all people and nationalities, in 2006, he founded the Eracism Foundation. Its mission is to eliminate racism, violence, and the disregard and intolerance of others. He especially wanted to create a program to give at-risk children the education and support they needed to grow in a diverse world and perpetuate the spirit of giving.

Louis Gossett Jr. is committed to his craft, but when asked for advice, he does not give acting tips or guidance. It is about understanding. Gossett spent his life giving to others, and his soundest advice is, "We'd better take care of ourselves and one another better. Otherwise, nobody is going to win anything. We need each other quite desperately for mutual salvation."

When reflecting on his life, he says, "It's been a good life, and I'll never stop acting—it beats regular work."

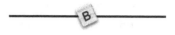

Of the more than 50 books I have written, at least 20 of them are fiction. Among these novels, nine of my stories, to date, have been made into movies. I remain convinced that if William Shakespeare, Mark Twain, or the apostle Paul were alive today—in addition to writing books— they would be making movies, as films reach a breadth of the population and touch people at a depth in their souls that books cannot approach.

When I began working with the creative production team that turned my novel *The Lamp* into an award-winning movie, I wasn't sure who would be best to play the pivotal role of the genie who would appear from a garage sale lamp. My first thought was to cast Barbara Eden. She was in her eighties at the time, and I thought it would be ironic and comical to contrast the memories people had of her as a young star in *I Dream of Jeannie* on television. When I met her to discuss the project, even though she was a senior citizen, she still retained the beauty and energy she'd had in her youth, which made her perfect as a Broadway star but perhaps not as appropriate for our movie.

My next thought was to get a physical comedian to play the genie, so I reached out to Tim Conway. While we had great conversations, and I remain a huge fan of his work, he didn't seem to bring the gravity to the part I felt it needed.

Finally, I thought I'd go in a completely different direction and get someone of great stature who exudes power, wisdom, and confidence. My mind leaped to the Academy Award-winning actor Louis Gossett Jr. After I met Lou and we bonded, he agreed that the part would be perfect for him, and he would be perfect for the project.

Working tirelessly for weeks on a movie set can be daunting, particularly if you have to deal with people who have elevated egos and entitled personalities. Mr. Gossett was approachable, down-to-earth, and available to the entire cast, crew, and even the interns working on the project. He brought his passion and energy to every moment of that film.

When you watch *The Lamp*, I would draw your attention to the scenes Lou did with Cooper, the dog. Cooper was the beloved pet of my treasured colleague Beth Sharp. Everyone loved Cooper, but he had no experience working on a movie. Most actors will tell you working with children or animals creates the most difficult conditions, but Lou was perfect. Cooper became a movie star, and the rest is history.

When I think of Louis Gossett Jr. and his powerful quote—"I think more important than law is the hearts of people"—I'm reminded that our accolades, fame, and fortune all fade into insignificance when compared to the way we touch people and impact their lives.

15

"Once you get rid of the idea that you must please other people before you please yourself, and you begin to follow your own instincts—only then can you be successful."

RAQUEL WELCH

RAQUEL WELCH was born Jo Raquel Tejada on September 5, 1940, in Chicago, Illinois, to Armando Carlos Tejada Urquizo, an aeronautical engineer of Spanish descent, from La Paz, Bolivia, and Josephine Sara Hall, who was an American citizen. She was named after her mother, Josephine, and her name Raquel originated in Spanish-speaking countries and was given to her to honor her paternal grandmother, Raquel Urquizo.

Internationally, Raquel Welch is recognized for her exotic Latin beauty, charm, and talent as an actress. Her brunette bombshell image filled the moviegoers' void left by losing Marilyn Monroe and other sultry actresses before her.

At an early age, she wanted to perform and entertain audiences. Following her dream, she appeared in nearly 75 action and comedy movies and various television shows throughout her career. In 1973, she won the Golden Globe Award for Best Actress—Motion Picture Comedy or Musical—for portraying Constance Bonacieux in *The Three Musketeers*. In 1987, she was nominated for a Golden Globe Award for Best Actress in a Television Drama for her role in *Right to Die*.

Raquel was voted one of *People* magazine's "100 Most Beautiful People in the World," *GQ* magazine's "25 Sexiest Women in Film," and *Playboy* ranked her third on their list of the "100 sexiest stars of the 20th Century." In 1995, she was chosen as one of the "100 Sexiest Stars in Film History" by *Empire Magazine*.

At 44, Raquel became an author. In January 1987, she released her first book, *The Raquel Welch Total Beauty and Fitness Program*, accompanied by an exercise videotape. She decided to write the health and fitness book while appearing on Broadway in the play, *Woman of the Year*.

"Every time I left the theater, there would be a crowd of women waiting to ask me questions, such as: 'What do you eat?' 'What kind of exercises do you do?' and 'How do you look like that?' Well, I wasn't about to stand there and explain my daily hour-and-a-half exercise routine or what I had for breakfast," she said. "I decided to take a year off to write. For the first time, I had a chance to get outside my image as an actress," she continued. "And for the first time, I had something to say."

In March 2010, she published her autobiography *Raquel: Beyond the Cleavage*. In it, she looks back at her life and talks woman-to-woman about her relationships, health, body image, career, family, forgiveness, and aging.

When Raquel Welch was two, her father, Armando, was transferred from Consolidated Aircraft Corporation in Chicago to General Dynamics in San Diego, so the family moved to California.

Two years later, her parents welcomed a son, James. Later, her sister, Gayle, was born into the family.

Throughout her childhood, there was tension in the household. Her father's volatile nature compelled her to find an escape by immersing herself in activities outside the home. She was mesmerized by the stories on the silver screen and found tranquility enthralling herself in movies and escaping to another world. She considered it a "transcendental experience."

Raquel also had a big dream of becoming a ballerina. From seven to 17, she took ballet lessons—until the day her instructor crushed her dream. Sadly, he said she did not have the body shape to become a professional ballerina. Disheartened, she turned to her second love—acting. It was a wise decision in hindsight.

As a schoolgirl, she came home one day and told her mother she was not particularly fond of the name Jo. She felt more comfortable with Raquel. So the next day, her mother went with her to school and asked the teachers to refer to her daughter as Raquel—she became Raquel Tejada. Most of the children in school found it difficult to pronounce her name, so they nicknamed her Rocky.

By 14, Raquel had won beauty titles, including "Miss Photogenic" and "Miss Contour." She attended La Jolla High School and was crowned Miss La Jolla. At the San Diego County Fair, she won the title Miss San Diego—the "Fairest of the Fair." She went on to win the state title of "Maid of California."

Academically, Raquel was a good student, graduating with honors. After graduating in 1958, she enrolled on a Theatre Arts scholarship at San Diego State. There, she performed in local theatre productions and found success. One year later, she won the title role in *The Ramona Pageant*, performed at the annual outdoor theatre in Hemet, California.

Soon after, Raquel found she was pregnant and married her high school sweetheart, James Welch, in May 1959. She gave birth to her first child, Damon, in November of that year, and in December 1961, the couple welcomed their second child, Latanne, whom they called Tahnee.

Raquel took a job as a San Diego weather forecaster at KFMB television, but soon she was overwhelmed juggling her many responsibilities with college, work, and children. She decided to leave San Diego State without completing her degree.

In 1962, she left the television station, and the couple separated for reasons undisclosed. She moved to Dallas along with her two young children and, for a short time, worked as a cocktail waitress and a model for the Neiman Marcus department store. She and the children returned to California in 1963. Ultimately, she divorced James in 1964 but retained the name Welch for her children and as a career choice to distance herself from her Latin heritage. Through the years, Raquel has reflected on her marriage, saying she should have worked harder to keep the family together.

A divorced mother of two young children, she dreamed of an acting career. She applied for roles with movie studios in Los Angeles, winning small parts in television programs and movies, such as *A House is Not a Home*, and the musical *Roustabout*, starring Elvis Presley. In 1966, she won a role in her first major film, *A Swinging Summer*. "When I first came to Hollywood, it was clear that no actresses really had children. So, I didn't really know which path my career would take."

In 1965, Fox Studios offered her a seven-year contract, and her career began to blossom. Initially, the studio executives asked that she change her name to Debbie, stating that Raquel Welch sounded foreign. Holding her ground, she declined, and Fox accepted her decision.

Her breakthrough movie was the 1966 science fiction film *Fantastic Voyage*. However, her minor role in *One Million Years B.C.* brought her to stardom.

Fox had lent her contract to the British studio Hammer Film Productions. She had only three lines of dialogue in the film, but the legendary doe-skin bikini she wore left a lasting impression. Instantly, she was recognized as an international sex symbol. The image became a best-selling poster. The poster's popularity continued through the years and was featured in the 1994 film *Shawshank Redemption*, starring Tim Robbins and Morgan Freeman. In the movie, Andy Dufresne, played by Robbins, hung the iconic poster over the hole he had carved out of the wall to make his successful escape from prison.

In addition to her starring movie roles, one-woman nightclub act in Las Vegas, books, and workout video, Raquel Welch has established financial success through her brand endorsements with Lux soaps, Foster Grant sunglasses ads, MAC skincare line, signature jewelry, and designer wigs. Her popularity also set the stage for the 1960s and 1970s fashion trends, and she, along with other well-known actresses, made the "big hair" style a popular trend.

Raquel has always played by her own rules, and in 1980, she starred in her musical television special, *From Raquel with Love*, showcasing her talents as an actress, singer, and dancer.

Married four times, Raquel realized that she was happiest being single. She first married James, and in 1966, she wed producer Patrick Curtis. They divorced in 1972. Her third marriage was to French-American television producer and journalist André Weinfeld in 1980. The marriage lasted ten years. In 1997, she married Los Angeles-based restauranteur Richard Palmer. The couple separated in 2008.

Raquel Welch has posed for countless publicity photos and impromptu pictures for fans. In 1979, she posed for *Playboy* but refused to pose fully nude. Hugh Hefner later wrote, "Raquel Welch, one of the last of the classic sex symbols, came from the era when you could be considered the sexiest woman in the world without taking your clothes off. She declined to do complete nudity, and I yielded gracefully. The pictures prove her point."

In speaking of her persona, she once said, "What I do on the screen is not to be equated with what I do in my private life. Privately, I am understated and dislike any hoopla." She said, "My family was very conservative, and I had a traditional upbringing. I was not brought up to be a sex symbol, nor is it in my nature to be one. The whole sex symbol thing is part of what I do as an actress. It's a kind of character I play. It's part of me, but not the whole me. The fact that I became one is probably the loveliest, most glamourous, and fortunate misunderstanding."

On February 15, 2023, after a brief illness, Raquel Welch died. She was 82. She reigns as one of America's most famous sex symbols, and for over five decades, she influenced the world.

I first encountered Raquel Welch when we were working on the movie *The Ultimate Legacy*, based upon my novel of the same title. I had written the character Sally Mae Anderson as a 99 year old woman reflecting back on her long and successful life. Initially, our thought was to have Lauren Bacall play the part. She was well into her nineties at the time and still had the power and presence to play the role. Unfortunately, her health was failing, and she was unable to appear in the movie. When the movie production team mentioned the idea of having Raquel Welch play Sally Mae Anderson, I literally laughed out loud.

I was looking for a stereotypical woman approaching her hundredth birthday, and even though she was in her mid-seventies, Raquel was still a vital and beautiful woman with much of the presence that had made her a worldwide, iconic sex symbol throughout her life. When I got to know her a bit, I realized she was more unlike her public image than anyone I had ever met. While she certainly understood what made her a superstar, and while she cultivated it over the years, Raquel Welch was intelligent, thoughtful, and very well-spoken.

Ironically, in our first conversation when I asked her how she had first started in the business, she told me she had been a weather girl in San Diego. For over 25 years, I have given a speech several times each year at a conference at a resort in San Diego. Due to the absolutely perfect weather year round, my opening joke to my audience had always been, "The most boring job in the world must be doing the weather in San Diego." I told Raquel she had ruined one of my standard jokes. She just laughed and told me to keep using the joke and add her to it, which I have done.

Her quote about pleasing ourselves as a way to success is particularly poignant coming from Raquel Welch, as for over half a century, she was a product of what people think of her. In the final analysis, Raquel Welch did a good job pleasing the world and pleasing herself, which made her an ultimate success.

16

"I was not naturally talented. I didn't sing, dance, or act, though working around that minor detail made me inventive."

STEVE MARTIN

STEPHEN GLENN MARTIN was born a "Wild and Crazy Guy" on August 14, 1945, in Waco, Texas, to Mary Lee Stewart Martin and Glenn Vernon Martin. His father, a real estate salesman and aspiring actor was stern and emotionally closed to his son, making the family dynamics strained for Steve and his sister Melinda. The pair were opposites, and unlike his father, Martin had a goofy jokester persona and wanted to make people laugh.

Steve Martin became a successful American actor, stand-up comic, producer, musician, comedic television writer, lyricist, and author of screenplays, novels, and children's books. He launched his stand-up comedy act and performed in small establishments before there were comedy clubs.

Known for his unconventional, absurd comedy routines and near-professional banjo performances, he has appeared before tens of thousands to sold-out theater and stage show audiences throughout the country.

When Martin was five, the family moved from Waco to Inglewood, California—his mother despised the Texas heat. Later they moved to Garden Grove, a mere two miles from Disney's first theme park, where he got his first job. His experience working at Disneyland may have set the stage for his lifelong love of entertaining audiences.

Martin launched his career in the 1970s and has won five Grammy Awards and a Primetime Emmy Award. He was awarded an Honorary Academy Award in 2013 for his extraordinary talents, unique inspiration, and contribution to the art of motion pictures. In 2016, he was nominated for two Tony Awards for his musical *Bright Star*. He received the Mark Twain Prize for American Humor, the Kennedy Center Honors, and the American Film Institute Life Achievement Award. Martin has starred in nearly 60 films, including: *The Jerk; Dead Men Don't Wear Plaid; The Man with Two Brains; Three Amigos; Planes, Trains and Automobiles; My Blue Heaven; Dirty Rotten Scoundrels; Parenthood; Father of the Bride* series; and *Cheaper by the Dozen,* to name a few.

Influenced by American banjo musician Earl Scruggs's rendition of "Foggy Mountain Breakdown," Martin taught himself to play the banjo at 17. With a friend's help, he played 33 RPM bluegrass records, slowed them down to 16 RPMs, and tuned his banjo so the notes would sound the same as the recording. He then was able to identify each note and play them perfectly.

"The only place to practice without agonizing everyone in the house was in my car parked on the street with the windows rolled up," he said, "even in the middle of August."

Later, Martin joined the country-rock group Nitty Gritty Dirt Band. He has played the instrument throughout his career, sometimes touring with various artists and bands.

The banjo became an integral component of Martin's 1970s stand-up comedy routine. In his 1981 final comedy album, *The Steve Martin Brothers*, he highlighted his stand-up genius on one side and his live performances with a bluegrass band on the reverse. His first solo album, *The Crow: New Songs for the 5-String Banjo* (2009), earned him a Grammy Award for Best Bluegrass Album.

He said of his musical talents, "It's not the music I was interested in, but the fun of moving my fingers across the strings."

Steve Martin's silliness and shtick may have started when he was ten. In July 1955, Disneyland opened its Anaheim, California, theme park two miles from his childhood home. With "no experience necessary" advertised for the position, he landed a job. For the next three years, he stood outside its gates selling twenty-five-cent Disneyland guidebooks. From morning to noon, weekends and summers, young Martin wore a candy-striped shirt, vest with a watch pocket, a flat-topped, wide-brimmed straw boater hat, and sported a bow tie. He earned a whopping two cents per sale—big money for a 10-year-old. Come noon time, he was free to roam the park, in uniform, as an official employee.

At 13, he outgrew the guidebook gig and was promoted to Frontierland as a trick-rope demonstrator selling lassos. What interested him, though, were magic tricks. His first real break into show business came while working at Merlin's Magic Shop in Fantasyland. There, he was allowed to perform magic tricks, which later became iconic elements of his stand-up comedy act that he created in his

20s and performed for more than 15 years. His ensemble included the classical arrow through his head, rabbit ears prop, and funny black glasses with a big fake nose. These were all items off the shelf at Merlin's.

Adding a burst of "happy feet," he sporadically surrendered to the music in his head and soul and danced about the stage ecstatically. His iconic expression, "Well, excuuuuuuuse me!" became a national catchphrase, and his comedy routine gave way to hilarity for audiences—young and old. Martin credits this expression to a Biloxi-born store manager named Irene, who favored the saying, "Well, excuse me for livin'!"

Expanding his act beyond Disneyland, Martin landed an occasional job performing for Boy Scouts, Kiwanis, and Rotary Clubs, allowing him to perfect his magic tricks, juggling routine, and balloon animal creations.

Martin also decided to audition his magic act to entertain at Disneyland's rival Knott's Berry Farm. He was hired and left Disney behind. At Knott's Berry, he joined the comedy troupe and performed comedic and other productions at "The Bird Cage" in front of paying audiences.

After high school, Martin was accepted at Santa Ana Junior College, where he enrolled in English poetry and drama classes. Unlike in high school, his quest to learn grew, and he became more interested in philosophy. Before long, he found that the junior college fell short of relevant classes and applied to Long Beach State College—later renamed California State University at Long Beach. There, he studied the philosophy of language, metaphysics, the history of ethics, and logic. Martin was ranked an A student.

While attending a psychology class, he read a study explaining the theory of comedy. Laughter results when the storyteller creates tension. Then, the audience's tension is released by delivering the punch line. He began to think, "What if I created tension and never released it?" He experimented with the concept and found that audiences selected their own release point. The idea worked, and he built his act based on that philosophy. It was the audience who chose what they considered funny.

Expanding his demographic reach, Martin moved from place to place, entertaining small audiences, frequently performing only blocks from UCLA. In 1967, he transferred to the university to study theater acting and television writing. By 21, he dropped out of college.

In 1967, his friend, Nina Goldblatt, used her influence to help Martin land a job as a staff writer for *The Smothers Brothers Comedy Hour*, which won him a Primetime Emmy Award for "Outstanding Writing for a Variety Series" in 1969. Writing for the show by day and sometimes appearing on it allowed him to perform his stand-up act at local bars and nightclubs at night.

While still attending college, Martin appeared twice as a contestant on the *Dating Game* television show that aired from 1965 to 1980. In his first panel appearance in 1968, Deana Martin, daughter of crooner Dean Martin, presented a series of questions to him and two other eligible bachelors to select one of the candidates for an all-expense-paid trip. Deana chose Steve Martin over the others, citing his desire to select the Goodwill store as the perfect location should he find himself trapped inside. The couple won a trip to Portofino, Italy.

In his second appearance on the *Dating Game* in 1970, the bachelorette was the real-life sister of Martin's childhood friend, Morris Walker. Using his clout as a comedy writer for *Smother's Brother's Comedy Hour*, he convinced the producers to bring his "long-lost" friend, Marsha Walker, onto the show, where he would be one of three bachelor contestants. The premise was that she would not know that one of the bachelors was her old friend, Steve Martin. Indeed, Marsha was aware, and the two planned the potential questions she would ask during the show. The result was as planned—Marsha chose Martin. Together they won an all-expense-paid trip to Tijuana, Mexico, to watch the bullfights. The trip inspired Martin's 1986 film *Three Amigos*.

Martin traditionally wore a dark suit and a then-fashioned wide necktie on stage. As his popularity grew, he began performing before sizable crowds, entertaining in arenas and stadiums with ticket capacities in the thousands. He no longer performed for empty bars and clubs but for 500-seat capacity rooms to 20,000-seat arenas.

With the house lights down and only a spotlight on him, Martin had to find a way to make himself more visible to ticketholders seated in the back or high up on balconies. His solution was to wear a three-piece white suit, a white shirt, and a black tie with a pocket scarf that illuminated in the spotlight. The brightness of his suit, along with his prematurely graying hair, appeared beacon-like to the crowd.

Martin released his first comedy album in 1977 called *Let's Get Small*. The album went platinum, selling over one million copies thanks to his performances on television shows. He appeared on *The Tonight Show, Starring Johnny Carson* 16 times. As one of the most successful guests on *Saturday Night Live (SNL)*, Martin appeared approximately 27 times and guest-hosted more than 15 shows.

Who could forget watching the musical parody "King Tut," written and performed by Steve Martin and accompanied by members of the Toot Uncommons (actually the Nitty Gritty Dirt Band)? Entertaining the *SNL* audience, Steve, dressed as Egyptian pharaoh Tutankhamun, sang and danced like an Egyptian.

Another famous skit on *SNL* was about the Czechoslovakian-born Festrunk brothers, Georg, played by Martin and Dan Aykroyd as Yortuk, emigrated to the United States in search of "swinging American foxes." The pair shimmied and sauntered in their plaid trousers, open print shirts, gaudy medallion chains, and newsboy caps, making audiences laugh time and again. They were "Two Wild and Crazy Guys."

Though Martin plays inept, witless, and arrogant during his performances, he bears no resemblance to the persona of his stand-up comedy act or the naïve and socially challenged characters he portrays in his movies and television. In reality, he is cerebral, shy, and articulate. He enjoys crossword puzzles, cats, art, computers, and especially lunch. "I'm not kidding. Lunch is very important to me," he said.

With his keen intellect, Steve Martin, a former California State University philosophy major, once considered being a college professor after becoming interested in the writings of the Austrian philosopher Ludwig Wittgenstein. In 1997, Steve Martin wrote in *The New Yorker* about his year-long efforts to get into MENSA, which originated from the Latin word meaning "table." The organization symbolizes the coming together of equals. MENSA's qualification for membership requires a person to score in the upper two percent of the population. With the average Intelligence Quotient score falling between 85 and 115, a score above 140 is considered a genius level. Martin's IQ is reportedly 142.

Steve Martin has spent his career in the spotlight but prefers to keep his personal life private. "In terms of who he is, not what he does, he's really very conservative," said longtime friend Terry DeLapp, a Los Angeles art dealer. Steve Martin is very old-fashioned and is the pinnacle of extreme politeness and sincerity.

In 1981, Martin stopped performing his stand-up comedy routine to concentrate on movies, saying, "My act was conceptual. Once the concept was stated and everyone understood it, it was done. It was about coming to the end of the road. There was no way to live on in that persona. You know, I didn't announce that I was stopping. I just stopped."

In 1984, while filming *All of Me*, he met the talented British actress, Victoria Tennant. The couple married in 1986. Unfortunately, it ended seven years later. In 2002, Martin met Anne Stringfield, a staff member for *The New Yorker*. Though they worked together on Martin's writings, they did not meet in person until a year later. In 2007, they invited friends and family to a party at their Los Angeles home. It was a surprise wedding, and guests were pleased to participate. The thirty-fifth Governor of Nebraska, Bob Kerrey, presided over the ceremony, with Lorne Michaels, creator and producer of *Saturday Night Live*, standing by Martin as best man.

At 67, Steve became a father, welcoming daughter Mary, in December 2012. In an interview for *AARP* magazine in 2017, he shared his thoughts on fatherhood, "I think if I'd had a child earlier,

I would have been a lousy father because I would have misplaced my attention on my career. I am very forthcoming with her, and it's great. She's given me way more than I've given her."

Still entertaining audiences in his 70s, Martin launched several national comedy tours with close friend and fellow comedian Martin Short. In 2018, the two released their *Netflix* special, *An Evening You Will Forget for the Rest of Your Life* and received three Primetime Emmy Award nominations. In 2021, he cocreated and starred in his first television comedy series, *Only Murders in the Building*, which aired on Hulu, alongside Martin Short and Selena Gomez, also earning three Primetime Emmy Award nominations, two Screen Actors Guild Award nominations, and a Golden Globe Award nomination.

Steve Martin has come a long way from the man who used to wear a trick arrow through his head. In speaking of his career, he said, "I feel very lucky in that I always knew what I wanted to do. There are people who are ten times smarter and more educated who really don't know, and I don't think you have a minute to spare."

Perhaps the best way to sum up his life is with his own words, "I really liked the longing, the dreams of wanting to be someone else, of wanting to burst into song and have a beautiful voice," he said. "In a very abstract way, that's what my act was about, a guy who wanted to be in show business. Perseverance is a great substitute for talent."

In 2010, he created the "Steve Martin Prize for Excellence in Banjo and Bluegrass Award," recognizing "a person or group who has given the board a fresh appreciation of this music, either through artistry, composition, innovation, or preservation and is deserving of a wider audience." The prize includes a bronze sculpture, $50,000, and a chance to perform live with Steve Martin.

As for his relationship with his father, at the end of Glenn Martin's life, father and son reconciled in their hearts the distance caused by Steve's success as an entertainer, and his sister Melinda grew to know her brother.

In a book filled with the highest and best thoughts of world leaders and historical figures, at first glance, Steve Martin might seem out of place. However, in the final analysis there may be no higher human calling than to share joy, entertain, and simply make people laugh. In his quote at the beginning of this chapter, Steve Martin acknowledges that he never felt talented or qualified for stardom in any way. This is a feeling shared by most of the award-winning actors and highly accomplished performers I have worked with on stage, television, and movies.

The myth of natural talent only emerges after a prolonged period of perseverance and stubborn tenacity. Steve Martin has made a career of finding unconventional ways to showcase his talent and leave us all laughing and entertained.

I believe all of us, especially entertainers like Steve Martin, should be judged not as much by who we are or what we do as we should be judged by the difference we make in the lives of others. In much the same way, no one has ever seen the wind, but you can look out the window and see the impact it is having on leaves, branches, and the world around you.

I have a dear friend and respected colleague who is a high-level corporate trainer and entrepreneur. I will never forget the occasion when she and I had the opportunity to screen Steve Martin's movie, *The Jerk*. She didn't simply like the film or even love it; she could literally recite every line of dialogue. When someone like Steve Martin uses their talent to impact someone you respect so much to that high of a degree, you have to simply stand back, applaud, and say, "Bravo."

17

"The greatest discoveries all start with the question, 'Why?'"

ROBERT BALLARD

ROBERT "BOB" DUANE BALLARD was born to Chet and Harriet Ballard on June 30, 1942, in Wichita, Kansas. An American retired Navy officer and Professor of Oceanography at the University of Rhode Island, he is best known for discovering the remains of the RMS Titanic ocean liner. "I wasn't a Titanic groupie," he said. "I read about it like everyone else and had seen the movie *A Night to Remember* (1958), but I wasn't fixated, so I didn't even think it would be a big deal." It turns out it was a big deal.

There is no shipwreck in the world more famous than the Titanic. Its discovery had been the dream of countless deep-sea explorers since the luxury White Star Line British steamship sank four days into its maiden voyage. The vessel, which stood as high as an 11-story building and nearly four city blocks long, left Southampton, England, on April 10, 1912, after stops in Cherbourg, France, and Queenstown, Ireland. It then set sail for New York.

Tragically, the RMS Titanic—"Royal Mail Steamer," indicating the ship was contracted to carry mail—struck an iceberg at 11:40 p.m. on April 14, 1912. The ship met its fate in the icy waters of the

North Atlantic Ocean 400 miles off the south coast of the Grand Banks of Newfoundland. Though the radio room and bridge crew received seven ice warnings throughout the day, there were no established procedures to follow. The warnings went ignored.

While a head-on collision was averted when the crew spotted the iceberg in the dark of the night, they had no idea that the berg had a jagged underwater spur that ultimately slashed a 300-foot gash in the hull below the 882-foot ship's waterline. The Titanic sank at 2:20 in the early morning of April 15, 1912. With a capacity to transport 3,300 people, 2,240 passengers and crew members were on board. More than 1,500 "souls" from all nations lost their lives in the disaster within three hours of striking the iceberg. A mere 700 passengers miraculously survived.

On September 1, 1985, the wreckage of the once-thought "unsinkable" Titanic was found in the dark depths below 13,000 feet of freezing water. "It reminded us," said Ballard, "that those legends of the great ship Titanic were real." Undersea explorer Robert Ballard documented his life, practically to the minute, with vast archives of his life and his work as an oceanographer.

Ballard was born six months after the Imperial Japanese Navy Air Service devastatingly attacked the United States Pearl Harbor Shipyard Naval Base in a surprise military air strike on December 7, 1941. After that, the Ballard family moved from Wichita to California to be near relatives, living two blocks from the Pacific Ocean.

At first glance, Robert and his brother, Richard, were frightened of the furiously splashing waves of the ocean, but once they became immersed in its waters, their fears left them. Ballard began to explore the tidal pools, discovering a new cast of characters daily—octopus, crab, or some other fascinating creatures that cycled in every 12 hours. Ballard found it a magnificent way to discover life in the ocean. Soon he explored the waters, beginning with snorkeling, then scuba diving deeper and deeper.

As a boy, Ballard did not find reading an easy task. He struggled, realizing that he had to read longer hours and with more focus to be at the same reading level as other children his age. "I didn't know I was dyslexic until I read the book, *The Dyslexic Advantage*. I remember when I read the book...slowly...I cried because it explained *me* to me for the first time," he said. "And now I've really embraced it. And I realize why I was able to do what I've been able to do because I'm such a vigil creature. I can imagine things in my mind, and it's perfect when I go down to the darkest depths; I look at my sensor systems, and I can form a mental image in a world of eternal darkness. I think it explains how I tick." It was through reading that Ballard realized his true passion in life.

The pivotal moment was when he was 12 and read Jules Verne's *20,000 Leagues Under the Sea*. Captain Nemo became his hero. But when Disney turned the book into a movie in 1954, he knew what he wanted to be when he grew up. There was a scene where Kirk Douglas harpooned a giant squid sea monster. He then went below deck and pushed some buttons, causing a window to open like the iris of the human eye. The actor peered out and saw Captain Nemo and his crew walking on the ocean floor. Before that time, Ballard had no idea that the ocean had a floor. He imagined there was only infinite darkness. When he shared with his parents his desire to become Captain Nemo, they did not laugh. They, too, imagined him going into the Navy or becoming an oceanographer.

Ballard followed his dream in 1959 by attending the Scripps Institute of Oceanography. He received his graduate degree in 1965 from the University of Hawaii Graduate School of Oceanography, where he trained dolphins and whales. Later, Ballard became a 2nd Lieutenant in the United States Army Intelligence. In 1967, he joined the Submersible Design Team at Ocean Systems Operations, North American Aviation. In 1974, he earned his doctorate in Marine Geology and Geographics at the University of Rhode Island Graduate School of Oceanography. He did this not to become a scientist but to fulfill his passion for the ocean.

As an Army officer in 1967 and while working toward his graduate degree, he received a letter from the US Navy saying he had six days to report for active duty at Woods Hole Institute of Oceanology in Massachusetts. He was assigned to the Office of Naval Research. He was no longer in the Army.

Ballard was appointed to man "Alvin," the first-ever underwater exploration vessel designed to extend first-hand knowledge of the ocean's depths. "Most of the planet has never felt the warmth of the planet and never will." He entered a world at depths of total darkness, and the experience changed his life.

Until then, no one had gone to the ocean floor to successfully prove the Theory of Plate Tectonics—the formation of continents where the Earth's outer shell divides into several plates that glide over rocky layers above its soft core. And no one had ever witnessed lava oozing out as the plates separated.

On the ocean floor, Ballard saw sea creatures that no one had ever seen, including the 13-foot-tall white worms that bled human-like blood and clams that were one foot across in diameter with no internal organs, mouths, or digestive tracks. These creatures exist through chemosynthesis—a chemical reaction providing energy sources—rather than photosynthesis—in which the sun provides its energy source. He witnessed a fluffy black substance bellowing from the ocean floor that appeared like "black smoke."

Initially, Ballard was prohibited by the Navy from sharing the fact that he had discovered the Titanic. "The Titanic was really a cover for a highly classified military operation to investigate two nuclear submarines that the United States lost during the cold war," he recalled. The operation intended to answer three questions: What are the nuclear reactors doing? What's the status of the nuclear weapons? Is there any evidence the Soviets have been there?

"The USS Thresher and the USS Scorpion, ironically, turned out to be on either side where the Titanic was lost. And, quite honestly, had that not been the case, you wouldn't be looking at the guy who found the Titanic," said Ballard.

The team learned from mapping and investigating the nuclear ship wreckage that both submarines imploded before they came to rest on the bottom of the ocean. On their way down, the pressure in the hulls created a massive explosion causing the submarines to blow apart. The team realized the heavy components had dropped to the ocean floor like a bowling ball, while the lighter mass created a long line of debris.

This theory held valid for the Titanic. The ship did not land where she went down, which is why other explorers could not locate the vessel. It was located at a depth of about 12,500 feet or 370 nautical miles.

Upon its discovery, in a powerful moment of silence, Ballard and his crew cheerlessly realized that they were hovering over the watery graves of the lost souls of the RMS Titanic.

"I didn't expect the world to go crazy. From the moment we passed through Nan Tucket Sound, the research vessel Knorr was cheered home." The headlines read, "Wreck of 'Unsinkable' Ocean Liner Titanic is Found" — *The Napa Valley Register,* and "Titanic Upright in Watery Grave" — *Tampa Bay Times.*

Ballard realized his life had changed. He was invited to countless press conferences by newspapers, journalists, and television talk shows, such as *The Tonight Show, Starring Johnny Carson. National Geographic Magazine* was eager to recount Ballard's discovery. One question frequently asked was, "Can the ship ever be raised?" According to Ballard, the ship was in superb condition, considering its longevity on the ocean floor. His answer, though, was, "Unfortunately, not." For more than a century, the oceanic environment, with its saltwater acidity, had deteriorated the vessel. To attempt marine salvage would compromise the ship's integrity causing it to crumble.

On discovering the location of the Titanic, his mother said, "He's done all these scientific things, but in the eyes of the world, I think he'll be remembered for the discovery of the Titanic." Ballard agreed, "Now they'll remember me for that rusty old boat. Moms are always right. I know my obituary has already been written, and regardless of what happens from this day forward, it will read, 'The guy who found the Titanic died today.'"

The RMS Titanic remains at the bottom of the ocean as a maritime memorial and scientific laboratory.

Among Dr. Robert Ballard's other accomplishments are his historic discoveries of hydrothermal vents, the German battleship Bismarck, and numerous other contemporary and ancient shipwrecks worldwide.

Robert Ballard became Captain Nemo.

Dr. Robert Ballard has a long, distinguished, and successful career spanning many projects, but he will always be linked to the Titanic. The Titanic is a reminder to us all that nothing is unsinkable. But on the other hand, nothing is undiscoverable.

In his quote, Dr. Ballard encourages us to always question, *why?* In our fast-paced, microwave world, we have a tendency to immediately think about *how, where, when,* and *who* before we contemplate anything else. Unless and until we answer the question *why,* everything else remains irrelevant.

Dr. Robert Ballard's work serves to remind us all that in the space age where everyone is focused on going farther and faster, there is much to be discovered here on earth and within the vast capacity of our own minds.

18

"I've been a survivor my whole life."

CHUCK WEPNER

CHARLES "CHUCK" WEPNER was born on February 26, 1939, in New York City, but he grew up in the low-income project housing in Bayonne, New Jersey. He became an American professional boxer. The 6-foot-5-inch, 230-pounder with a long-arm reach ranked as a heavyweight in the boxing industry. He was known as the "Bayonne Bleeder" for his ability to take a solid punch and remain standing, albeit with the inevitable result—massive facial cuts that bled profusely.

In his boxing career, Wepner knew how to energize audiences and put on a gripping display in the ring. In 1964, he became the national Golden Gloves champ, and his life as a heavyweight boxer inspired the 1976 film *Rocky*—he was "the real Rocky Balboa." Without the Bayonne Bleeder, there would be no "Italian Stallion."

During his career, Wepner boxed against some of the greatest heavyweight champions in history. Most famously, they included Muhammad Ali in a 1975 championship fight, Randy Neumann in multiple bouts resulting in two wins and one loss, and a match in 1973 against 6-foot-6-inch-tall Ernie Terrell, who had held the

World Boxing Association's heavyweight title from 1965 to 1967. In June 1970, he was the last to fight the former undisputed world heavyweight champion, Sonny Liston. The fight left Wepner with a fractured cheekbone, broken nose, and 72 stitches.

His fight with Sonny Liston earned him the nickname the "Bayonne Bleeder." Liston's jabs left Wepner's face badly beaten, and he could hardly see through the blood gushing from the cuts above both eyes. Rosie Rosenberg, then editor of the *Jersey Journal*, was ringside sporting a stylish brown suit. By the night's end, her charming garment was stained with Wepner's blood, as his crimson fluid had sprayed into the audience with every blow to his face. The referee stopped the fight in the ninth round. The next day's headline read, "Bayonne Bleeder Loses to Liston." Therein was his forever nickname, though he never liked the tag. Sadly, Charles "Sonny" Liston died six months after the fight in Las Vegas.

In his career, Wepner fought 51 fights with 35 wins, of which 17 were declared knockouts, and two were draws to Everett Copeland in 1964 and 1965. He lost only 14 competitions in his career. While most of his boxing events were held in the United States, he fought in Japan, Puerto Rico, England, and South Africa.

Chuck Wepner grew up in the streets of Bayonne, New Jersey—the roughest of neighborhoods. He lived with his mother and grandparents in an abandoned coal shed until he was 13. "This was a tough town with a lot of people from the docks and the naval base, and you had to fight to survive," he remembered.

When he was eight, some of the townspeople held public bouts called "Smokers" because the spectators filled the air with billowing clouds of cigarette smoke. The event required young boys to put on oversized trunks and boxing gloves and spar with each other. This training introduced Wepner to his lifelong interest in boxing.

Just out of high school in 1959, the motion picture *Battle Cry* motivated Wepner to join the United States Marine Corps. The film depicted the early days of America's involvement in World War II. A Marine battalion struggled through boot camp, physically trained themselves into great shape through intense exercise, and fought the enemy. According to Wepner, "The lightning was all the women that they attracted. Back then, not like today, joining the armed forces still seemed glamorous." He, too, wanted glory and a few pretty girls, so he joined the crash crew. His job was to put out fires and save pilots who had crash-landed. In a 1975 *Sports Illustrated* article, Wepner was credited with saving the lives of three Marine pilots during his military career by pulling them from their fiery airplanes.

While serving in the Marines, he became a member of the boxing team. This assignment afforded him more to eat, extra weekend passes, and additional workout time in the gym. He earned a reputation for being able to withstand a powerful punch and endure more pain than his fellow Marines. While stationed at one of the airbases, he was named military champion.

At 20, Wepner was discharged from service. By then, he was a husband with one child and another on the way. According to his mother, there would be no leisure or stretch of relaxation before earning a living for his family. She secured a job for him, working the midnight security shift at Western Electric. To supplement his income, he moonlighted as a bouncer at nightclubs. But no matter where he went, fights seemed to follow him. "I was undefeated in bathrooms, telephone booths, and alleys," he said.

While working at Tony Meda's nightclub in Bayonne, the Police Athletic League boxing coach approached him in need of a Golden Gloves heavyweight. Wepner thrived at boxing and became the national Golden Gloves champion, fighting in dimly lit boxing holes that drew only a couple thousand people.

Though he earned little money from fights after he paid his manager and corner man, his celebrity status more than made up for the thrashings he endured. "I started becoming famous," Wepner said, "And started liking boxing a little better." What he liked was waking at 5:30 each weekday morning to train. He ran five miles through Bayonne's Hudson County Park, went to his job at Allied Liquors, ate dinner at home in the evening, and headed to Bufano's Gym to train as his final routine of the day.

In January 1975, the wild-haired boxing promoter Don King offered Wepner the chance to fight heavyweight champion, Muhammad Ali, "The Greatest" of all time, for the heavyweight championship. It seemed like a random match-up and, perhaps, an easy win for Ali. King aimed to keep Ali in shape and primed for an upcoming high-profile, high-paying fight with George Foreman. He did not want Ali to be seriously challenged, but selecting Wepner was King's mistake.

Muhammad Ali was known for his trash-talking, spoken-word poetry, and rhyme scheme banter. Not to be outdone, Wepner composed a predictive poem titled *Goodbye Ali, Hello Chuck*. It went like this:

I know they say you're the greatest to ever wear the crown,

And that this is a fight of little renown.

But tomorrow night, you are going to run out of luck.

There will be a new champion, and his name will be Big Chuck.

The match was intense. In the ninth round, Wepner hit Ali squarely under his heart. It knocked the champ off his feet, and he was down for the count—so Wepner thought.

Immediately, Wepner turned to his corner and said to his manager Al Braverman, "Al, start the car. We're going to the bank. We are millionaires."

Looking over Wepner's shoulder, Braverman said, "You better turn around. He's getting up, and he looks mad."

In a flurry of fierce punches, Ali opened cuts above both of Wepner's eyes and broke his nose. He left his opponent gasping for air. Ali's wrath did not let up, and the longer Wepner took a beating, the more the spectators shifted their loyalty to the underdog. They stopped chanting "Ali, Ali" and began cheering "Chuck, Chuck." The remaining rounds were brutal for Wepner.

Ultimately, Ali knocked him down in the 15th round with 19 seconds left. The referee counted to seven before calling the match a technical knockout. Though Muhammad Ali outboxed the Bayonne Bleeder from New Jersey, Wepner became world -famous.

That night, struggling actor and screenwriter Sylvester Stallone had watched the match live on closed-circuit television at a Philadelphia theatre. He was in awe of Wepner's endurance and his refusal to fall. He listened in amazement as the crowd supported the dark horse. Stallone realized that there was a story to be told. For the next several days, he penned the script for what would become the highest-grossing motion picture of 1976—*Rocky*. The movie earned more than $117 million at the box office, and Sylvester Stallone became a renowned star and an international action hero.

Stallone never denied that Wepner was the film's inspiration. He invited Wepner to audition for a part in Rocky II, but he did not win the role or profit from any of the *Rocky* movies' success. Though he remained a liquor salesman and stopped boxing, Chuck Wepner lived the life of a boxing champ. He went to nightclubs and accepted party invitations, never saying "no."

"You get caught up in the partying and celebrity," Wepner said, "And you do a lot of stupid things."

In 1976, Wepner went up against 7-foot-5-inch, 463-pound wrestling legend "André the Giant" at Shea Stadium in New York. The Giant vs. Chuck Wepner match was the headliner of a WWWF pro wrestling exposition labeled the "Showdown at Shea." During the match, André had taken a full-faced jolt from Wepner, and the formidable Frenchman picked Wepner up and tossed him out of the ring. Wepner lost the fight.

One day, his buddy Artie Stock, a nightclub magnate, saw a huge, furry animal named "Victor the Wrestling Bear" at a convention and suggested to Wepner that he have a go at him. According to Wepner, he would not have wrestled just any bear, but this was a world-famous, 8-foot-6-inch tall, 1,250-pound world-famous celebrity bear who had appeared on the *Ed Sullivan Show*. Victor might have been the most formidable contender of his career. He fought the bear not once but twice—for charity. The first exhibition benefited the Make-a-Wish Foundation, bringing in $30,000 in charitable contributions. The second bout brought $25,000 to support the St. Jude Foundation.

In one bout, Wepner began throwing jabs at the muzzled and de-clawed animal when the bell rang. Not realizing the bear was not trained to take punches about the face and nose, Wepner continued aggravating the animal. Victor became demented and retaliated. He reared up on his hind legs and roared ferociously. The bear rushed Wepner, picked him up, and threw him 15 feet into the air. When Wepner spun around to get up, he found the bear was on top of him. The trainer blew the whistle, and Wepner realized the bear was trying to kill him.

Chuck Wepner's last boxing match was on September 26, 1978, against professional newcomer Scott Frank for the New Jersey State Heavyweight Championship. Wepner lost the fight in round 12 and announced his retirement soon afterward.

By the mid-1980s, Wepner had developed a cocaine habit. In 1985, he was convicted of conspiracy to distribute cocaine and served 17 months of a ten-year prison sentence. After serving his time, he returned to Bayonne, and, to his surprise, the community welcomed him back, and Allied Liquors restored his employment.

In addition to inspiring *Rocky* films, Chuck Wepner's life events were chronicled in the movie *Chuck*, and he was the subject of the 2019 sports film, *The Brawler*.

Chuck Wepner is credited for putting Bayonne on the map, and in 2022, a 2,500-pound statue of Wepner was unveiled in Dennis P. Collins Park, Bayonne, New Jersey. At the ceremony, actor Liev

Schreiber, who portrayed Wepner in the movie *Chuck*, described him as "a guy who fought his own demons harder and better than anyone else."

Addressing the boxer, he said, "I am so proud and so grateful to you for letting me have your story."

During his career, Wepner held the World Boxing Association North American Boxing Association heavyweight title.

Twice divorced, Wepner lives with his third wife, Linda, and is considered an expert in consumer liquors, wines, and spirits. He is still the busiest sales representative.

"I've been a survivor my whole life," he said.

Of my 50 books, nine of them have been turned into movies, and I remain an avid student of the filmmaking process. I frequently screen movies I admire and listen to the optional director's commentary as the movie plays. I've always respected Sylvester Stallone and what he has done as a creative force in the motion picture industry both in front of and behind the camera. During his commentary as part of the original *Rocky* movie, he mentioned Chuck Wepner, the famous fight with Muhammed Ali, and Wepner being the real Rocky.

I remember regretting that I never got to meet or talk with Chuck Wepner. Then one of my talented and industrious colleagues discovered that Chuck Wepner was 83 years old and still working every day from his home in Bayonne, New Jersey. I sent him some of my books and movies along with a letter requesting an interview. We actually had two lengthy interviews, and I hope to get to speak with Mr. Wepner again.

I've had the privilege of interviewing many high-profile actors, businesspeople, and athletes. Many of them are disappointing once you get behind the thin veneer of their fame, but Chuck Wepner was everything I'd hoped he'd be and more. While he may not have been the greatest fighter of all time, or even the best in his era, I believe Chuck Wepner may have gotten more out of his talent than any other boxer.

Talking with Chuck Wepner is a little like talking with Sylvester Stallone playing Rocky. Everything is borderline humorous with a lot of wisdom and perspective behind it. When I asked him about any advice he might have as he looks back on his long and colorful career in boxing, he immediately went to his fights with the bear.

Mr. Wepner said, "Whatever you do, don't ever hit a bear in the face."

As an author, speaker, and columnist, I'm always looking for universal advice that can apply to anyone in any situation. Chuck Wepner's wisdom about not hitting a bear certainly fills the bill.

On a more serious note, during our interview, he described going to prison as the best thing that ever happened to him as it changed his thinking, helped him overcome his addiction, and gave him a powerful perspective for the future. When I asked Chuck Wepner how he wanted to be remembered, he told me he wanted people to think of him as a guy who always gave 100 percent, and anyone who bought a ticket to a Chuck Wepner fight got their money's worth.

When it's all said and done, you and I can do little more than recognize the key moments in life, seize them, and give 100 percent of our effort.

19

*"The secret to so many artists living so long is
that every painting is a new adventure."*

NORMAN ROCKWELL

NORMAN PERCEVAL ROCKWELL was born in New York City, New York, on February 3, 1894, to Jarvis Waring Rockwell, an office manager in a textile firm, and Anne Mary "Nancy" Rockwell, a parent who was often ill. As an American painter and illustrator, his work portrayed innocence and centered on family values. He had an eye for detail and became a legend with paintings that humorously depicted the American dream in simple, relatable scenes from everyday life. Each image told a masterful story as he imagined life in the Midwest that projected little change or struggles.

"Without thinking too much about it in specific terms, I was showing the America I knew and observed to others who might not have noticed," he said. "They are life slides through which dreams are projected."

His art conveyed the nation's tapestry of the times, giving prominence to freedom, tolerance, common decency, and democracy.

In his later life, his paintings depicted more somber world issues. They became socially and politically charged as he became more aware of life's inequalities and the nation's push for civil rights and liberties. An example of this social shift is evidenced in his 1963 *Look* magazine cover titled *The Problem We All Live With*. It represents the story of six-year-old Ruby Nell Bridges, the first desegregated African-American girl attending the all-white William Frantz Elementary School in New Orleans on November 14, 1960. The painting shows the child being escorted to school by US Marshalls, awakening us to art's importance in our changing society.

For more than 50 years, Rockwell created magnificent, colorful covers for *The Saturday Evening Post*, at that time a weekly magazine. His best-known included soldier *Willie Gillis* in a series of 11 paintings produced at the height of World War II. The paintings followed the young soldier's military career from his US Army induction to his discharge. Another notable work was his 1943 female industrial worker, *Rosie the Riveter*. In 1951 his Thanksgiving cover titled *Saying Grace*, depicted a woman and her young son saying grace over their meals at a diner while other patrons observed.

Rockwell did not particularly enjoy growing up in New York. At six, he would perch on the rooftop of his boarding house and look down at the Irish and the German gangs fighting each other in the streets with bicycle chains. It left him sadly emotional. The images in his mind significantly impacted him and stole his childhood innocence. One memory of the city that stayed with him was witnessing a drunken woman beating a man with an umbrella. She was screaming as she stumbled through a parking lot.

"Against that image of the city, I set the country. The view of life I communicated in my pictures excludes the sordid and the ugly. I paint life as I would like it to be," he explained.

Throughout his childhood, Rockwell felt lonely, though he had the company of his older brother, Jarvis Waring Jr., and his parents. His family was not particularly close. He displayed no athletic abilities, nor did he possess a high scholarly aptitude.

Summing up his self-image as a boy, he once wrote, "I didn't think too much of myself, a lump, a long skinny nothing, a beanpole, without the beans. All I had was my ability to draw."

As an adult, Rockwell was described as pigeon-toed, hollow-chested, and bore narrow shoulders. He carried all of 135 pounds on a lanky six-foot frame and was rarely seen without his iconic Dunhill pipe pressed tightly between his teeth, packed with his favorite American burley mixture. The sweet, aromatic notes of cocoa filled the air. The blend is still available, with his famous *Fishing* painting replicated on the tin.

Rockwell wanted to be an artist from an early age and found acceptance within his peer group, for they admired his drawings. At 14, he transferred from high school and enrolled in illustration classes at New York's Chase School of Art, initially named for painter and teacher William Merritt Chase. In 1910, he attended the National Academy of Design before enrolling in the Art Students League.

His early works were produced for *St. Nicholas Magazine* and the youth publication *Boy's Life*, the official magazine of the Boy Scouts of America. While still in his teens, Rockwell was appointed its art director and continued his affinity with the Boy Scouts throughout his life.

He commissioned his first illustration before his 16th birthday, designing a set of Christmas cards. By 18, Rockwell owned a studio, and he contracted with Carl H. Claudy to illustrate his book *Tell Me Why: Stories about Mother Nature*.

Norman Rockwell once told the story of the special box, which looked like a small funeral vessel, he had built to carry samples of his work to present to the editors of *The Saturday Evening Post*. He was happily surprised when the *Post* hired him to produce the front covers for the magazine. For the next 47 years, Rockwell painted covers for 321 issues, calling it "the greatest show window in America."

Though not officially recognized as a historical period of the arts, the years between 1850 and 1925 marked the "Golden Age of Illustration." American periodicals found they could cheaply produce a wealth of information and entertainment through imagery by mass-producing works of art in magazines and on covers. Rockwell had a distinct talent for storytelling through his paintings.

On May 20, 1916, *The Saturday Evening Post* recognized his abilities when they showcased the 22-year-old's red and black toned painting titled *Boy with Baby Carriage*, for which Rockwell earned $75. In those days, the magazine only produced red and black tone covers. The picture was a humorous depiction of boyhood that featured three young boys. One boy was dressed in his Sunday best, sporting a baby bottle in his lapel pocket, and pushed a baby in a wicker carriage as he strolled past two ballplayers dressed in baseball uniforms. The boys mockingly tipped their caps at the scowling fellow as he went about his babysitting chore.

Rockwell married Irene O'Connor that same year, but by 1921, his five-year marriage ended. Downhearted, he moved to Alhambra, California, at the invitation of an old friend. While there, he met and married schoolteacher Mary Barstow in 1930. She was 14 years his junior and a year out of college. Soon, the couple returned to Rochelle, New York, and over the next several years, had three children—Jarvis Waring, Thomas Rhodes, and Peter Barstow. The family moved to Arlington, Vermont, in 1939.

In his work, Rockwell used live models and incorporated authentic props to aid in his imagery. Approximately 200 of his family, friends, and townspeople had posed for his paintings. Rockwell's first wife, Irene O'Connor, was featured in his painting *Mother Tucking Children into Bed*, published on the cover of the *Literary Digest* in January 1921. Director Steven Spielberg used Rockwell's painting in his 1987 coming-of-age war movie, *Empire of the Sun*, starring Christian Bale. Spielberg reenacted the picture with actors in the scene when they put the character Jim to bed in the first act. In his 1948 painting *Happy Skier on a Train*, the onlooking woman in the upper right-hand corner is his second wife, Mary. To create the piece, he had genuine train seats shipped to his Arlington studio.

On May 15, 1943, a fire destroyed Norman Rockwell's Arlington, Vermont, studio when he knocked out the contents of his pipe onto a cushion. Thirty years of history went up in smoke, destroying props and costumes that were the foundation of his work. He lost a collection of a lifetime. It is believed that some were unseen works from the 1920s and 1930s. Initially, the loss of his paintings and historic props devastated Rockwell. Still, he realized that the tragedy gave him the freedom to rededicate himself to his craft and an opportunity to start afresh.

In 1953, Rockwell and his family relocated to the picturesque New England town of Stockbridge, Massachusetts. His wife Mary had suffered mental illness for years, and the move brought her closer to the psychiatric hospital Austen Riggs, where she received proper care. At times throughout his life, Rockwell suffered from bouts of depression. He also received treatment from the institution's analyst Erik Erikson, who told biographer Laura Claridge, "He painted his happiness but did not live it."

Rockwell had dreamt of being a household name through his paintings. At 42, he created his 1943 *Four Freedoms* series after hearing Franklin D. Roosevelt's 1941 "Four Freedoms" State of the Union speech in which the President referred to the fundamental human rights of Americans that the government should protect. Rockwell's paintings titled *Freedom of Speech*, *Freedom of Worship*, *Freedom from Want*, and *Freedom from Fear* matched the eloquence of FDR's words.

After the paintings appeared on separate covers of *The Saturday Evening Post*, the publication received millions of reprint requests. The United States Postal Service began issuing postage stamps, posters, and other marketing materials with the images. The government used them to promote its War Bond drive to aid in the war efforts by forming a successful touring exhibition to raise money. The tour helped to raise $132 million, and Norman Rockwell became the household name he had always dreamt of being. By the end of World War II, the Office of War reported that it had printed four million posters of the *Four Freedoms*.

Married almost 30 years, on August 25, 1959, his beloved Mary died of a heart attack. Two years later, Rockwell married his third wife, Mary Leete "Mollie" Punderson, a retired Milton Academy English Teacher. With Mollie's influence, Rockwell's social and political awareness grew. He began taking on a more somber depiction of world issues in his paintings.

After *The Saturday Evening Post* published his last cover in 1963, Rockwell spent the next ten years producing paintings for *Look* magazine. His progressive views on the Civil Rights movement and world poverty projected strong emotion in his art.

In 1966, Rockwell's Stockbridge studio was located, for a brief time, on Main Street above "The Back Room," better known as Alice's restaurant. It was owned and operated by the boarding school librarian Alice Brock. Singer-songwriter Arlo Guthrie's 1967 song "Alice's Restaurant" is based on the true story of his visit to Stockbridge, Massachusetts, when he spent Thanksgiving dinner at Alice's home along with some friends. After dinner, he and his friends offered to haul away some garbage for Alice. Subsequently, he was arrested for littering when someone discovered an envelope with his name printed on it among the rubbish. The restaurant ceased operation in April 1966.

In his lifetime, Norman Rockwell produced more than 4,000 original works. He illustrated over 40 books, including Mark Twain's *Tom Sawyer* and *Huckleberry Finn*. He was commissioned to paint portraits for United States Presidents Dwight D. Eisenhower, Lyndon B. Johnson, Richard M. Nixon, and Ronald Reagan. His most famous presidential portrait was of John F. Kennedy, with a somber and thoughtful expression on his face. Other celebrities included

Judy Garland and Colonel Harland Sanders. Rockwell also created advertisements for companies such as Coca-Cola, Jell-O, General Motors, Scott Tissue, and others.

In 1976, two years before his death, Rockwell donated his home studio and its contents to the Norman Rockwell Museum. The building was cut into two parts and moved to its current location in Stockbridge, Massachusetts, in 1986.

President Gerald Ford presented Rockwell with the Presidential Medal of Freedom in 1977, saying, "Artist, illustrator, and author Norman Rockwell has portrayed the American scene with unrivaled freshness and clarity. Insight, optimism, and good humor are the hallmarks of his artistic style. His vivid and affectionate portraits of our country and ourselves have become a beloved part of the American tradition."

A year later, on November 8, 1978, Norman Rockwell died of emphysema at his Stockbridge, Massachusetts, home, leaving behind his wife, Mollie, and his three boys. He was 84.

"The story of my life," Rockwell once said, "Is really the story of my pictures and how I made them because, in one way or another, everything I have ever seen or done has gone into my pictures."

At one time, Rockwell's paintings were considered the most expensive ever sold. His 1951 *Two Plumbers* sold at auction for $13,100,000 in 2017, and his *Which One?* depicting an undecided man in a voting booth, was auctioned for $6,537,500 in 2016.

In 2008, Norman Rockwell was named the official state artist of Massachusetts. Most of his works can be viewed at the Norman Rockwell Museum.

As a blind person myself, I experience art and artists in a different way. While their work may not impact me directly, I experience the impact their work has on others. Many artists travel around the world to bring us images of strange and unusual sights and scenes. Norman Rockwell used his art to hold up a mirror and allow America and Americans to know themselves better.

His work brought significance to everyday life and brought attention to causes, making him a true change agent. He lived his life with passion and left the world with enduring images of hope, values, and significance.

In his quote, "The secret to so many artists living so long is that every painting is a new adventure," Norman Rockwell reminds us that when we can find our own passion and share it with the world, we can live long, healthy, and happy lives.

20

"My songs are the door to every dream I've ever had and every success I've ever achieved."

DOLLY PARTON

DOLLY REBECCA PARTON was born on January 19, 1946, in a two-room cabin with no electricity, no indoor plumbing, but lots of music and loads of faith, on the Little Pigeon River in Pittman Center, Tennessee, a six-square-mile town located in East Tennessee near the foothills of the Great Smoky Mountains National Park. As a young girl, her family moved from Pittman Center to a nearby Locust Ridge farm, where she experienced most of her treasured memories.

Dolly Parton became an iconic American singer-songwriter, actress, philanthropist, businesswoman, and creator of the Dollywood Foundation, which includes her Imagination Library Foundation. The organization provides books to children from newborns to five-year-olds. The legendary Queen of Country Music has entertained audiences through her music and film careers spanning more than six decades.

Parton has written over 3,000 songs, with 25 number-one hits, surpassing other female performers. Seven of her albums have topped the country charts, and she has sold over 100 million records worldwide. Among Dolly Parton's most notable hits were her favorite, *Coat of Many Colors*, which was adapted into a motion picture about her life, *Jolene*, inspired by a red-headed bank teller in Nashville who once had a crush on her husband Carl, *9 to 5*, written for the motion picture of the same name, and *I Will Always Love You.*

Dolly Parton has won countless awards for music and acting, and in 2018 she achieved two *Guinness World Records*—"US Hot Country Songs Chart with Most Hits by a Female Artist," totaling 107, and "Most Decades with a Top 20 Hit" on the "Billboard's Hot Country Songs Chart," with a total of six. She has earned 11 Grammy Awards, her 2011 Lifetime Achievement Award, and 51 Grammy Awards nominations throughout her career. She is the second most nominated female artist for the prestigious award. Dolly has won ten Country Music Awards, three American Music Awards, seven Academy of Country Music Awards, and two Academy Award nominations. In 1999, she was inducted into the Country Music Hall of Fame.

Dolly Parton was the fourth of twelve children born to Robert Lee "Widner" Parton Sr., and Avie Lee Caroline Owens Parton, who married at ages 17 and 15. By ages 37 and 35 and 20 years of marriage, the couple had experienced 11 pregnancies, producing twelve children—the last was a set of twins. To pay the mountain doctor's fee for Dolly's delivery into this world, her parents traded Dr. Robert Thomas a sack of cornmeal for his services.

Fourteen people living in close quarters was a challenge. "It was crowded!" Dolly said, "With that many brothers and sisters, there was plenty of teasing and fighting, but we were all in it together."

Her mother sometimes became overwhelmed with the daily household chores and nurturing responsibilities. So when a new baby came along, Avie assigned a special role to an older sibling to care for the new little one. It was their responsibility to take charge when their mother was busy. At age nine, Dolly was responsible for the ninth child to come along. Dolly named him Larry Gerald, but to her devastation, the baby died four days after birth. Once always singing, the Smokey Mountain songbird went silent in her time of mourning.

The Parton family lived in extreme poverty. Her father sought work on construction jobs to supplement the meager income he received from his small tobacco farm.

"We were poor, but I never felt poor. We always had food, a roof over our heads, and clothes on our backs. It wasn't exactly what we wanted, but Mama and Daddy were always quick to point out the families that suffered far more than we did. It all seemed just natural to me," she said.

The tiny cabin had sizable cracks in the walls, and the cold, windy winters brought plenty of snow that blew through openings in the floorboards and settled like pinstripes on the shanty floor. Always cold in the wintertime, the nights were more so. The children slept snuggled three or four to a bed. Sleeping with many people in one bed was not necessarily bad. They all kept toasty warm—until one of the little ones wet the bed.

The farm acreage and the surrounding woodland where she grew up inspired her song, *My Tennessee Mountain Home*. Subsequently, the farm was sold, but in the late 1980s, Dolly repurchased it.

The Parton family was a musically gifted clan, and their talents for singing, songwriting, and playing musical instruments were inherent in their mother's family, the Owens. Though all of the Parton children were talented, Dolly took her gift of music to a level that surpassed them all.

"There's 12 of us kids, six girls and six boys, and we all sing and write and play," she said in a 2010 interview. "It's just that I think I've taken it farther. I don't know that I'm near as good as some of the others, but I've been more willing to sacrifice and work a little harder than some of the others might have been willing, you know, to do just because they wanted to have a family and do other things. But there's a lot of talent in this family."

Showcasing their phenomenal voices, the family sang at the Pentecostal church every Sunday, where her grandfather, Jake Owens, was the preacher. Dolly began singing in the choir at six.

At seven, she began playing a homemade guitar, and at eight, her mother's brother, Bill Owens, gifted her first real guitar. It was a Martin Model 5-18, the smallest guitar made by Martin Guitars. Dolly referred to it as "Baby Martin." Dolly clanks and strums her acrylic nails together like a musical instrument when a guitar is not on hand. When asked about composing her hit song, *9 to 5*, she said, "When I actually wrote this song, I used my acrylic nails on the set... because they make noise and sound like a typewriter to me."

Dolly made up songs before she could write and performed them for family and friends in her home. Forever an extrovert and willing to show off her talent, she was happy to entertain them. When they had visitors, her mother would say, "Go on, Dolly, grab your guitar and play that song you wrote."

Uncle Bill recognized Dolly's talent as a child and helped develop her musical career. "He saw early on that I was serious about my singing," Dolly said. Bill, an entertainer, was born in 1935 and began performing in the 1950s in East Tennessee as "Little Billy Earl with the Spit Curl." He mentored Dolly throughout her career and was her rock. He taught her chords and encouraged her to continue singing, writing songs, and playing her guitar. He took her to Nashville, approximately 200 miles from her home, to promote her singing at various venues. Over time, he took her to record labels and publishing companies to pitch songs.

Initially, Dolly Parton's success came as a songwriter, frequently collaborating with her uncle. Together, they wrote many songs—music and lyrics. Her first single, "Puppy Love," released in 1959 on the small Louisiana label Goldband Records, was the first song she and Uncle Billy cowrote. She was merely 11.

Dolly's songs have been recorded by many artists, including Bill Phillips's *Put It Off Until Tomorrow*, which won the 1966 BMI Song of the Year award, and the 1967 Top 10 hit *Fuel to the Flame*, recorded by Skeeter Davis. Other well-known artists to record her songs were Kitty Wells, Hank Williams Jr., and countless others.

When she signed with Monument Records in 1965, they pitched Dolly as a "bubblegum pop" singer and released singles such as *Happy, Happy Birthday Baby*. Her genuine passion was for country music, though the record company did not believe it suited her high soprano voice. Eventually, the record company granted her wish to record country genre.

In 1956, at age ten, Dolly performed regularly on *The Cas Walker Show* in Knoxville and on local television and radio shows. At 13, she made her debut at the Grand Ole Opry. It had always been her dream to be on that stage, and she could not have been more thrilled when Johnny Cash introduced her that night. She was immediately charmed by him. Sharing advice, Cash encouraged her to follow her instincts regarding her music career.

All of her notoriety, unfortunately, created jealousy among her schoolmates, and she was bullied at school occasionally.

At 18, the day after Dolly graduated from high school in 1964, she moved to Nashville to chase her dream of country music fame. That day she met her future husband, Carl Dean, at Nashville's Wishy Washy laundromat. While she waited for her laundry to wash, she took a stroll outside. Along came Carl in his truck and hollered to her, "You're gonna get sunburned out here." She said something clever, smart-aleck-like, and he asked her for a date. On their first date, he took her home to meet his mother. He suggested to his mom that she feed Dolly because he planned to marry her.

Two years later, the couple married, though her manager insisted they wait at least one more year so that she could concentrate on her career. They ignored his advice and eloped across the Tennessee border to Georgia to avoid the wedding announcement being published in Tennessee newspapers. After they married, the couple bought a farm in Nashville and took in several of Dolly's siblings to raise. Affectionately, family members gave them the lifelong nicknames "Aunt Granny" and "Uncle Peepaw."

Carl has never gone on tour with Dolly and has seen her perform live only once. A homebody, he tends to the farm by grating the roads, keeping the grass mowed in the backfields, and working on tractors and old trucks. In 2016, Dolly and Carl celebrated their 50th wedding anniversary.

Dolly has always taken pride in her iconic beauty with her towering blonde wigs, plunging neckline, perfectly applied nails and makeup, and five-inch high-heeled shoes to compensate for her small stature. Her secret to keeping her waistline thin is her high-protein diet and portion-control meals. But her secret to appearing slender on stage is due to the placement of her wireless microphone pack. Unlike many singers who keep their packs concealed at the back of their waist, Dolly keeps hers in a specially designed compartment in her wig. She fears that positioning it on her waist may make her waistline appear bulky.

Openly, Dolly Parton admits she has had some surgical cosmetic work done over the years, saying, "If I see something sagging, dragging, or bagging, I get it sucked, tucked, or plucked." When fans ask about her appearance, she says, "Well, it ain't cheap. I just look cheap. It's just a lot of good doctors, you know, a lot of good makeup." Dolly sees herself as being in show business, much like a show dog or a show horse. "I have to kind of keep it all groomed and clipped," she giggled. "I'd have been six feet tall if I hadn't gotten so bunched up at the top."

In an interview, she explained where her look originated. "There was this woman—I grew up, first of all, way back in the mountains. We only got to go to town every once in a while. But every time we would, there was this woman that was the town trash. But I thought she was beautiful. I didn't know what any of that meant. I just see this woman with yellow hair piled on her head and bright red lipstick, red nails, high-heeled shoes, and I thought she was the prettiest thing I'd ever seen. Mama would say, 'Oh, she's just trash.' And I thought to myself, 'That's what I want to be when I grow up—trash.' I thought that was the word for how she looked. So, I grew up to look just like her."

Even as a child, young Dolly put methylate and mercurochrome on her lips and darkened her eyebrow with burnt kitchen matches by licking them and applying the ash as a dye. In the summer, she used pokeberries mixed with water to create rouge. Though people began to think she was a jezebel, she assured them she was not. "There was no way," she said, "I didn't want nobody to mess up my makeup or smear my lipstick." Dolly has taken what she considers tackiness and gaudiness into an art form. She does not apologize for that or anything else.

Dolly is careful not to be seen outside her iconic look when on tour. Before she began touring in her custom bus, she stayed in hotels. Just in case of a fire, earthquake, or calamitous event that would take her from her hotel room in the middle of the night, she slept in her makeup, kept her wig perched on a lamp next to the bed, and positioned a pair of high-heeled shoes within reach.

As a style choice since 2010, Dolly wears only long-sleeved gowns and costumes and dresses each up with a matching pair of custom-made, sometimes jeweled, gloves during her performances. Admittedly, Dolly also has tattoos covering scars from previous procedures and surgeries. "I do have a few little tattoos, but they were mostly done to cover scars because I'm so fair," she said.

In 1967, Dolly was invited to join the syndicated television show, *The Porter Wagoner Show*, replacing "Norma Jean" Beasler. At first, she was not highly accepted, as Norma Jean's fans loved her dearly.

Over time, Dolly won the viewers' hearts, and she and Wagoner became an iconic duet. Dolly spent eight years on *The Porter Wagoner Show* before pursuing a solo career. Though at the opposition of Wagoner, she felt she owed it to her career. To ease Wagoner's pain over losing her, she went into his office and sang her 1974 song, *I Will Always Love You*, written as a farewell to her business partner. It captured her appreciation for him. She recorded the song, which went to number one on the country chart. On tour, it has become her signature closing song.

Ultimately, Porter Wagoner sued Dolly for breach of contract, and the two remained estranged for many years. In 2007, they reconciled. On October 28 of that year, Wagoner died of lung cancer. Dolly was with him the day he died, saying, "I held his hand, and we prayed."

In 1975, after hearing *I Will Always Love You*, Elvis Presley wanted to record it. His manager, Colonel Tom Parker, invited Dolly to the studio to meet Elvis before the taping. She thought it was the most exciting thing to have happened in her career. The day before the recording session, Parker called to inform Dolly that for Elvis to sing her song, as a rule, she must relinquish 50 percent of the publishing rights.

Dolly recalled telling Parker, "Well, it's not my rule. I hate this more than you could even imagine, but I cannot give you half the publishing. I just can't do it, and I won't do it. *I Will Always Love You* had been a number-one song with me already. It was the most important song in my catalog."

The disappointment brought tears to her eyes, and she was sure Elvis was disappointed, too. "I don't blame him for asking, but I don't blame me for saying no," she said. Later, Priscilla Presley told her that Elvis sang the song to her as they left the courthouse after their divorce. Over the years, *I Will Always Love You* has been recorded by several artists, but Whitney Houston ultimately immortalized it.

Many years later, Dolly came across an old cassette tape while shuffling through her archives. On it were three songs that she wrote back-to-back. She discovered that she wrote *I Will Always Love You* on the same emotional night as she composed *Jolene*.

Aside from her television career, Dolly has starred in many movies, including *9 to 5* (1980), *The Best Little Whorehouse in Texas* (1982), *Rhinestone Cowboy* (1984), *Steel Magnolias* (1989), and the story of her life titled, *Coat of Many Colors* (2015).

Dolly credits her musical abilities to her mother but her excellent business sense she owes to her father. "I can sit in a room with the biggest businessmen, and I don't feel a bit inadequate. In fact, I always feel like I got a little something on most of 'em," she admits. When she decided to fulfill her dream of opening her theme park, Dollywood, her attorney, and others believed it to be a bad idea. Today, Dollywood is a reality.

Through her Dollywood Foundation, headquartered in Sevierville, Tennessee, she remains committed to helping the people of her hometown. In 1986, she opened Dolly Parton's Dollywood theme park in Pigeon Forge, Tennessee. Dollywood is the largest employer in Sevier County, employing approximately 4,000 people, including many of her siblings and their families. The theme park has brought millions of dollars to the local economy through tourism. A replica of the Parton's Locust Ridge cabin is featured at Dollywood for guests to tour and witness her humble beginnings.

Inspired by her father's illiteracy, in 1995, Dolly initiated her Imagination Library, also part of the Dollywood Foundation. Since its inception, more than two million children have been registered, with 172 million books distributed free throughout the United States, Canada, Australia, Ireland, and the United Kingdom. "I created the Imagination Library as a tribute to my Daddy," Dolly posted on her website, "He was the smartest man I have ever known, but I know in my heart his inability to read probably kept him from fulfilling all of his dreams." For this gesture, Lee Parton was most proud of his daughter.

The Dollywood Foundation has also helped to raise funds for cancer research, rehabilitation, treatments, and various HIV/AIDS-related charities.

In March 2022, Dolly Parton collaborated with James Patterson, releasing their novel titled *Run Rose Run*, about an aspiring country singer trying to shake her dark past and make it big in the Nashville music business. Dolly knew the best way to contribute to the project was to write songs—lyrics and music—based on the characters they had chosen for the novel. Kicking it off, Dolly wrote the lyrics and sent them to Patterson, who then expanded the story and characters. In the meantime, Dolly recorded the songs on an album by the same name.

Dolly Parton always believed she would become a star. That is exactly what she became. Dolly credits her Uncle Billy for her success, saying, "It's really hard to say or to know for sure what all you owe somebody for your success, but I can tell you for sure that I owe Uncle Billy an awful lot." Uncle Billy died in 2021 at 85.

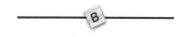

In this book and in the previous volume of *Words that Shaped Our World*, my coauthor, Kathy Johnson, and I have endeavored to feature some of the greatest and most notable people and their words. We tried to limit each notable figure to a brief chapter, but Dolly Parton and her life defy brevity. This chapter is among the longer ones we have written, and we left quite a bit out to get to this point. If you wrote Dolly's whole life in a novel or a screenplay for a movie, it probably wouldn't work because the reality is so unbelievable. Many people have lived the proverbial rags to riches story, but few of them have started out as ragged or ended up as rich, in every way, as Dolly Parton.

In Dolly's quote at the start of this chapter, she reminds us that she stays in touch with her roots and the songs that brought her fame, fortune, and stardom. While Dolly Parton's life and career may seem hectic and chaotic at first glance, if you really study it, you will come to understand that she built one success on top of another to create a monument to her talent, hard work, and spirit. Dolly Parton's career has brought joy to millions, and her philanthropy has made the world a better place.

21

*"I've done just about everything I've ever
thought or even didn't think I would do. Making
people laugh is all I care about."*

BOB NEWHART

GEORGE ROBERT "BOB" NEWHART was born on September 5, 1929, in Oak Park, Illinois, the second and only boy among the four children born to George David Newhart, a part-owner of a plumbing and heating supply company, and Julia Pauline Burns Newhart, a housewife. Once going by his given name George, like his father and grandfather, as his career took off, he became known as Bob.

Bob Newhart became a legendary American stand-up comedy veteran famous for his deadpan comedic delivery. He is recognized for his keen wit and detailed observations of human nature, and he turns everyday situations into comedy routines that make people laugh. Jack Benny, his late friend and role model, once said, "A comic says funny things, but a comedian says things funny."

Bob considers himself a comedian, and his talents skillfully transitioned into a successful acting career, starring in 17 movies and owning four television sitcoms, each containing all or a portion of his name in the title.

Newhart won numerous awards, including a Golden Globe, an American Master by PBS Television, three Grammys, the TV Land Icon Award, and a Primetime Creative Arts Emmy Award. In 2002, he won the prestigious Mark Twain Prize for American Humor, presented by the Kennedy Center. His comedy albums have sold more than 1.1 million copies worldwide. In 1993, he was inducted into the Television Academy Hall of Fame; and in 1999, he received a star on the Hollywood Walk of Fame.

His authentic and iconic stammering style of storytelling and his involuntary sentence pauses throughout his jokes enhance the impact of the punchline. It is what keeps his audiences riveted about what is to come next.

"Tension is very important to comedy, and the release of the tension," he said, "That's the laugh."

As he often points out, stammering is not the same as stuttering. "Stutters have trouble with the letters, while stammerers trip over entire parts of a sentence." When asked about his stammering comedic delivery in an interview, he said, "I mean, I never said, 'Oh...oh, look, nobody's doing a stammer; I think I'll do it. What a great opportunity.'"

But his spasmodic repetition and mild manner of clean comedy have set him apart from other comedians. Like Benny, he is unafraid of silence or hesitations in his routines. It enriches the joke.

Raised in a strong Roman Catholic household, Newhart attended the Loyola University of Chicago after graduating from the all-boys Saint Ignatius High School. He graduated in 1952 with a Bachelor of Science in business management, focusing his studies on accounting. After returning from a two-year stint in the US

Army, he enrolled in Loyola University's School of Law on the G.I. Bill, beginning a path to becoming a lawyer.

Newhart envisioned life as a trial lawyer, believing it would enable him to use his acting experience from Saint Ignatius, where male and female roles alike were played by boys, combined with his exceptional wit to wow jurors and judges alike.

On his law school journey, he interned for a wage garnishment law firm operated by a trio of brothers. One day, one of the partners asked him to appear on their behalf before a judge and request a court continuance on a case. Newhart refused, noting that he was not yet a lawyer and that to portray one was unethical. Ultimately, he left the firm and law school. With his academic responsibilities in the mornings, his afternoon duties as a law clerk, and performing with the Oak Park Players theatre group at night, he realized something had to give.

Nevertheless, Newhart considered the year and a half well spent. The silver lining, he said, was that "Law school did give me an appreciation for the precise word. Lawyers have to nail every phrase or constantly be in danger of an adversary exposing a loophole." Another essential lesson he learned about being a lawyer—he should never become one.

In 1952, before law school, he was drafted into the US Army and served stateside during the Korean War. His undergraduate degree and IQ test results made him eligible to attend the officer training school. He declined when approached with the opportunity, knowing he would return to civilian life after his two-year stint.

As an inductee, the Army flew him to Camp Roberts in California for boot camp. It was his first flight on a plane, and throughout his life, he expressed his discomfort with flying. "I take white-knuckle flights. I have a couple of drinks before, a couple during the flight—and then I sit there and suffer." Later, Bob banked on his fears by writing a side-splitting routine called "Grace L. Ferguson Airline and Storm Door Company."

Once he completed basic training, Newhart was assigned to the Army's personnel management group and traveled up and down the West Coast auditing records at military installations. For Newhart, the work was more about comfort and entertainment than the job. As a traveling auditor, bases in nicer climates seemed to have the darndest trouble with their records.

"We'd be scheduled for three days, but upon arrival, we would send word to our warrant officer that things were a mess, and we'd need at least a week to straighten them out," he said.

In smoldering hot weather, though, the records miraculously appeared spotless, and the team finished in a day. Private, non-commissioned officers' quarters were provided as a safeguard when the team claimed to carry top-secret material.

It took Newhart several years to settle on a lifelong career. In high school, his first job was working at the Austin-Madison Bowling Alley, a half block from his home. He worked as a pin spotter for two years, four hours every night. Earning ten cents per round, which equated to approximately $6 a night, Newhart manually set the pins upright for the next roll. Inevitably, when a strong bowler threw the ball, the pins and bowling balls flew his way haphazardly. It was a dangerous job for a young boy. Though growing up, he pictured himself as a successful kegler, a career bowler with a 170 average score was far from professional quality.

In 1956, Newhart's first real job was in the engineering department at US Gypsum, which manufactures wallboard and drywall. There, he worked as an accountant for a year until the company offered him a full-time position in Poland Springs, Maine, and asked that he relocate. Newhart refused. Instead, he resigned and accepted a bookkeeper position in the accounting department for the Glidden Company in downtown Chicago, responsible for reconciling the books between the company's operating divisions. He was also responsible for reconciling the petty-cash drawer against the daily receipts.

While the end-of-day totals were always close, they never seemed to balance. At five o'clock, everyone in the department headed home, but Newhart frustratingly worked hours into the evening trying to find the petty cash discrepancy. After a few weeks of irritation, he devised his own accounting theory. It was simply the "That's close enough" method, in which Newhart pulled the exact amount needed to reconcile from his pocket and placed it into petty cash. He no longer wasted hours trying to find mistakes. Over time, he would discover that the petty-cash drawer had an overage, so he merely pocketed the amount in excess. In the end, between the petty cash and his pocket, he reconciled the account daily.

Several weeks into this new accounting practice, Mr. Hutchinson, the head of accounting, realized his system for balancing petty cash and approached him. "George," as he was called in his early career, "These are not sound accounting principles."

Newhart responded, "You know, Mr. Hutchinson, I don't think I'm cut out for accounting because this makes absolutely perfect sense to me. Why would you pay me $6 an hour to spend three or four hours finding a $1.40? It's much easier if I just make up the difference out of my own pocket because I'll get it back next week."

As in becoming a lawyer or professional bowler, it was apparent that accounting was also not a strong suit.

In 1958, Newhart quit accounting and accepted a position as an advertising copywriter working under Fred A. Niles, a major independent film and television producer. At Fred Niles, Newhart learned about the world of film and television.

For laughs and to pass the time not having to reconcile petty cash anymore, Newhart would call his coworker, Ed Gallagher, in the afternoons. They entertained each other with comedic phone calls and engaged in funny banter. Newhart identified himself as various characters, such as a plant manager for a yeast factory or an airline pilot, and he made up hilarious exchanges and absurd comedy routines. Ed, always the straight-man interviewer, swapped funny lines and engaged in improv routines.

Another friend, Chris Petersen, heard their comedy routines and offered to invest in and promote them in exchange for a share of the profits. This gesture convinced Newhart and Gallagher that their phone conversation skits were worth promoting, so they recorded 100 demo tapes and mailed them to radio stations around the country, hoping for airtime. To their surprise, they sold their comedy on contract to three radio stations—one station each in Florida, Idaho, and Massachusetts—for a mere $7.50 per week for five minutes of sketches. Their only expense was acetate tapes and postage. Everything was going well until one of the stations refused to pay. Soon, they realized they were losing money and declined to renew the contracts for the other two stations.

As it turned out, Gallagher accepted a job as an advertising executive in New York and moved his family out of Chicago. Newhart was left with the radio recording business. Though the duo was unsuccessful, it was an unlikely beginning to a long and successful comedy career.

Gallagher's void forced Newhart to adapt his routines, creating the familiar one-sided conversations he became well-known for in his comedy. In due time, it seemed the copywriting business did not suit Newhart any better than becoming a professional bowler, a lawyer, or an accountant. Incidentally, Newhart was fired after six months of employment.

At that point, "I made the decision that I was going to try comedy, and if it didn't work, then I knew it didn't work," he said. "Then I would go back and do whatever. But at least I wouldn't torture myself the rest of my life, wondering whatever would have happened."

Fame as a comedian did not find Newhart overnight. Now that he had free time, he spent it refining his stand-up routines and writing comedy material with the understanding he had nowhere to perform an act. To supplement his income, Newhart worked part-time at places such as Goldblatt's, Abercrombie & Fitch's subsidiary V, L & A, and the Illinois State Compensation Board. At that time, he had no intention of getting a full-time job, though it was offered to him many times.

With the help of his friend and popular Chicago disc jockey Dan Sorkin, Newhart landed an audition as a DJ for a radio station in Grand Rapids, Michigan. Though he had no experience in radio broadcasting, the station sent him into a sound booth and gave him a commercial script to read. He was nervous and kept mispro-nouncing words. Before long, he began laughing throughout the demo, but no one noticed him. When he completed the recording, he wasted no time leaving the building. He had failed miserably and never heard from the station again.

Sorkin liked Newhart's style of comedy and invited him to appear on his radio show performing his famous "Abe Lincoln vs. Madison Avenue" routine. The humorous routine involved a one-sided con-versation with Abe Lincoln from his press manager's perspective before Lincoln's Gettysburg Address. This performance led to the producer of the *local* Emmy Awards inviting Newhart to perform it in the lobby of the Chicago Tribune Building. After seeing his act, anchorman Alex Dryer hired Newhart to appear on a man-in-the-street radio program to lend comic relief by playing different characters being interviewed. This job led to Newhart occasionally landing work doing voiceovers and commercials.

Furthering Newhart's success, Sorkin, who had listened to some of Newhart and Gallagher's taped routines, shared them with the head of talent at Warner Bros. Records. In 1959, the company signed Newhart to a recording contract. This deal came before he had even performed stand-up in front of an audience. Warner Bros. wanted the album performance recorded live at a nightclub, but owners were not enthusiastic about booking unfamiliar head-liners. So, finding a club that would bring Newhart on stage took nearly a year. Ultimately, the Tidelands Motor Inn in Houston, Texas, changed Newhart's life forever. His first comedy album, *The Button-Down Mind of Bob Newhart*, performed live on stage at the Tidelands, was released on April 1, 1960.

He recalled, "When I first started out in stand-up, I just remember the sound of laughter. It's one of the great sounds of the world."

Newhart's act became the first comedy album to hit number one on the Billboard Mono Action Album charts. This success brought him immediate sell-out status in nightclubs and theaters throughout America. It was a hit, bolting to number one, where it remained for 14 weeks. That year, the album won a Grammy for Album of the Year. His second album, *The Button-Down Mind Strikes Back*, was as successful as the first. The two maintained the number one and two spots on the charts for nearly 30 weeks.

Initially, Newhart did not understand the meaning behind the title, "The Button-Down Mind," and asked Warner Bros. Records to explain. It responded that many of the routines on the albums related to marketing, the media, or television. At that time, everyone working on Madison Avenue wore button-down collars, so that became the inspiration to connect to the masses. To Newhart's surprise, the album went wild, and he went from merely the man on the street to an overnight success—though overnight took a year and a half of hotel stays and nightclub performances, in reality. The album's success led to an invitation to appear on what was to become one of the longest-running primetime variety shows in television history—*The Ed Sullivan Show*.

Before long, Bob Newhart became a household name. Fame brought immense opportunities. Adding to his success, he recorded seven more albums, each culminating in a multi-platinum project. Besides winning a Grammy Award for Album of the Year for *The Button-Down Mind of Bob Newhart* on April 13, 1961, he won a Grammy Award for Best Comedy Performance—Spoken Word for his follow-up album *The Button-Down Mind Strikes Back!* His third Grammy was awarded for Best New Artist.

For the next 12 years, Newhart traveled from venue to venue, making people laugh with his stammering-style delivery. In 1961, his success landed him a hosting job on the 60-minute variety program, *The Bob Newhart Show*, but it was short-lived. Though airing only one season, it earned him a Peabody Award and a Primetime Emmy Award nomination for Outstanding Achievement in the Field of Humor.

In 1962, Newhart met the love of his life. His friend and fellow comedian Buddy Hackett decided that his babysitter, Virginia "Ginnie" Quinn, was dating a man unsuited for her. He thought Newhart would be a perfect match and set them up on a blind date.

"I've got a girl for you," Hackett said. "She's going with another guy, but I don't think he's right for her, so I'm going to fix you up on a blind date. You'll meet her, and you'll date, and you'll get married. Then you'll have kids, and you'll call one of the kids Buddy."

It turned out that Newhart was a more appropriate suitor. On their first date, he took Ginnie to dinner. Though he had already eaten, he watched as she dined—and spilled mayonnaise on her purple dress. The date went reasonably well, and they began dating briefly.

On his 32nd birthday, Ginnie broke it off. She was seeing someone else. A short time later, Newhart called Ginnie. They talked and decided to give it another go. At the time, though, he was preparing to go to St. Louis for a performance and asked her to accompany him. Ginnie, being no stranger to showbiz, was the daughter of Bill Quinn, who played Mary Tyler Moore's father on her weekly television show, and he had a role in *Star Trek V: The Final Frontier* as David McCoy. She understood the lifestyle of an actor.

"My parents would never let me go with you to St. Louis," she said.

Offering a chintzy proposal, he asked, "What if you had a ring?"

They selected a suitable engagement ring the next day, and Newhart made the proposal official.

On January 12, 1963, they were married.

Before walking down the aisle, her father said, "Sweetheart, I can still get you out of this."

After the reception, Bob steered his wife into the passenger side of the Ford Thunderbird she encouraged him to buy. The problem was that Newhart had never bothered to get a driver's license. Up to this point, he never needed one. There were always planes, trains, and cabs to rely on when traveling. But in the face of the wedding guests, it would be embarrassing for his new bride to drive them. Instead, he got behind the wheel, winging it. Ultimately, Newhart got a driver's license, and being that everyday life inspired the comedian's routines, perhaps this experience influenced his famous routine, "Driving Instructor."

Bob Newhart's first movie role came in 1962 with *Hell is for Heroes*, a World War II drama. Other movies include *Hot Millions* (1968), where he played an annoying software specialist; *On a Clear Day You Can See Forever* (1970), as Dr. Mason Hume; the satirical war comedy *Catch-22* (1970), playing the crazy military Major whose first, middle, and last names are Major; and the satirical dark comedy *Cold Turkey* (1971), playing the role of advertising executive Merwin Wren. In 1977, he was the voice of Bernard, the plump young mouse in the Disney animated feature *The Rescuers* and the 1990 sequel, *The Rescuers Down Under*. In 1997, Newhart played the beleaguered school principal, Tom Halliwell, in the comedy *In & Out*. In *Legally Blonde* and *Legally Blonde 2: Red, White, and Blonde*, Newhart portrayed doorman Sid Post.

In 2003, Bob Newhart starred in the timeless and magical Christmas tale *Elf* as Papa Elf, who adopts a human baby, played by Will Farrell, at the North Pole. "We knew that casting Bob would be an iconic, timeless choice," said director Jon Favreau. "I always loved his deadpan delivery."

Like viewers watching *It's a Wonderful Life* every holiday season, *Elf* has become a holiday tradition.

In 2006, Newhart's memoir, *I Shouldn't Even Be Doing This! And Other Things That Strike Me as Funny*, was published. It became a *New York Times* bestseller.

Newhart may be best known for his six-season sitcom *The Bob Newhart Show*, which aired from September 1972 to April 1978. Newhart portrayed psychologist Dr. Robert Hartley, who lives in Chicago with his wife Emily, played by Suzanne Pleshette. The weekly television show allowed Newhart to get off the road touring and spend more time with his family.

In each episode, the line "Hi Bob!" was repeated time and again. The phrase occurred so often that students at Southern Methodist University in Dallas, Texas, developed a drinking game in the show's syndication. Each time someone said, "Hi Bob," they all consumed a drink.

The game became a phenomenon. Even *Saturday Night Live*, hosted by Bob Newhart in February 1995, created a hilarious "Hi Bob" sketch starring Chris Farley and Chris Elliott. In the backstage setting, as fellow cast and crew passed Newhart and uttered the familiar phrase "Hi Bob," the pair took a shot of what appeared to be alcohol, unbeknownst to Newhart, and they quickly became inebriated. Before long, the two were well beyond walking a straight line.

Newhart got his next big situation comedy show *Newhart* in October 1982, playing Vermont innkeeper Dick Loudon alongside Mary Frann as his wife, Joanna. The show ran until May 1990, culminating in an all-time best series finale. In the last episode, Dick and his wife remain in the inn, even though the whole town has been turned into a golf course. The inn gets bombarded with golf balls, and Dick is hit in the head. It knocks him unconscious. Dick wakes to realize it has all been a dream.

"It was my wife's idea," Bob said. "We were going to a Christmas party, waiting in line to get a picture taken, I said to my wife, 'I think this is going to be my last year.' ...She said without a second's pause, 'You ought to end the show in a dream sequence because there are so many inexplicable people: Larry, Daryl, and Daryl were right out of *'Deliverance!'*"

The night of the final taping, two years later, the *Newhart* cast and crew, who were privy to the ending, kept it a secret. The audience went wild when the studio lights came up for the last scene. They instantly recognized the comforter on the bed before them from *The Bob Newhart Show*.

When the excitement subsided, Dr. Robert Hartley sat up in bed and said, "Honey, you won't believe the dream I just had."

To the audience's surprise, Emily turned the light on, sat up, and said, "That settles it. No more Japanese food before you go to bed."

To add to the humor, Bob told Emily, "You know, you should really wear more sweaters." Dick Loudon's wife, Joanna, always wore fashionable sweaters.

Bob Newhart starred in two more television shows, *Bob* (1992-1993), playing a cartoonist, and *George & Leo* (1997-1998), portraying a bookstore owner. During his career, Newhart appeared on many television shows, such as *The Librarian*, *Hot in Cleveland*, and *The Big Bang Theory*, to name a few, and he appeared on numerous interview programs. In the absence of Johnny Carson, Newhart guest-hosted *The Tonight Show* 87 times.

In 1991, his alma mater, Loyola University, merged with Mundelein College, where his three sisters graduated. In their honor, in 2012, the Newhart Family Theatre at the Mundelein Center for the Fine and Performing Arts opened at Loyola University in Chicago.

Experiencing a health scare in 1985, Newhart realized his wellness was deteriorating. He had been a heavy smoker for more than 30 years, and in every photograph of him, he was holding a cigarette. One day, he developed a severe nosebleed that would not stop and required medical attention. He was diagnosed with secondary polycythemia, which is a condition that produces excess red blood cells and increases the risk of stroke. With the help of a patch, he quit smoking within weeks.

Bob Newhart has spent more than six decades traveling around the world entertaining audiences. He has earned the good fortune to spend time with the people he loves. Unfortunately, Newhart has lost many close friends in his lifetime.

"This time of life, to go look in the Rolodex and see how few people are left, that's...that's tough," he said. "Because when you get down to it all, it's all about family and friends."

Newhart has outlived many television comrades, including Suzanne Pleshette, Bill Daily, Marcia Wallace, Mary Frann, Tom Poston, Peter Scolari, and Jack Riley. In 2017, he lost his closest and dearest friend, Don Rickles. Most importantly, on April 23, 2023, he lost his beloved wife, Ginnie. She died in Los Angeles after a long illness.

Bob and Ginnie Newhart were married for sixty years and shared four children, Robert, Timothy, Jennifer, and Courtney, and ten grandchildren. Though none of the children were officially named "Buddy," the couple called one of their daughters Buddy.

"I've always said, 'I don't care how successful you've been in this business, if you haven't had a good family life, what have you really achieved? Not an awful lot," Newhart said.

When asked how his marriage had lasted so long, he said, "The marriages of comedians, no matter how stormy, seem to last a long time, and I attribute it to laughter. No matter how intense the argument you're having, you can find a line, and then you both look at each other and start laughing. It's over, you know? I think that sense of humor is very important to the longevity of a marriage."

Newhart loves the sound of laughter, which is why, well into his 90s, he still performs occasionally.

"I don't think I'll ever stop performing. It's in my blood," Newhart said.

Bob Newhart has proven that laughter is still the best medicine.

In 1977, I began my college career, and I was trying to determine what subject I wanted to study and earn my degree. Psychology had always seemed somewhat fascinating but a bit mysterious, obscure, and unapproachable. Then, throughout the mid-1970s, Bob Newhart came into our home every week as a psychologist. It was fun, upbeat, and humorous. Bob Newhart's comedy made it seem like we were laughing along with his patients and not at them. I completed degrees in psychology and sociology. Those degrees became the basis of my life's work as an author, movie producer, speaker, and columnist.

In my book *The Ultimate Gift* and the movie based upon it, I attempted to identify 12 of the most important aspects in life that a grandfather would want to pass along to his grandson. In addition to the gifts of work, money, friends, and family, I identified laughter as a critical element of a successful life.

Out of all the things Bob Newhart has accomplished in his nine decades of life thus far, he identifies laughter as the only thing he really cares about. Newhart has given us the gift of humor throughout his life, and he will leave a legacy of laughter for generations to come.

22

"Most of us end up with no more than five or six people who remember us. Teachers have thousands of people who remember them for the rest of their lives."

ANDY ROONEY

ANDREW "ANDY" AITKEN ROONEY was an award-winning American journalist, essayist, syndicated newspaper columnist, and television writer best known for his cantankerous yet humorous commentaries on the weekly broadcast *A Few Minutes with Andy Rooney*. From 1978 to 2011, he was part of the CBS News program *60 Minutes*, and his commentary aired at the end of each weekly episode. Rooney reported on his experiences, observations, and opinions—usually complaining about the things people already thought about and detested themselves.

"I obviously have a knack for getting on paper what a lot of people have thought and didn't realize they thought," he once said. "And they say, 'Hey, yeah!' And they like that."

Rooney was born on January 14, 1919, in Albany, New York, to Walter Scott Rooney and Ellinor Reynolds Rooney. He had one sister, Nancy Reynolds Rooney, four years his senior. Rooney attended the Albany Academy, an independent college-preparatory day school, for six years. There, he began his writing career as a contributor to the student magazine *The Cue* before enrolling at the private liberal arts college, Colgate University, in Hamilton, New York, where he served as editor for Colgate's magazine *The Banter*. He played on the school's football team and developed a life-long affection for the game. His formal education ended with the emergence of World War II in 1941.

At 22, he was drafted into the US Army and sent to Fort Bragg, North Carolina, for basic training. Soon, his unit, the 17th Field Artillery Regiment, shipped out to Europe. In 1942, with a bit of education behind him and a limited amount of Army writing experience, he was assigned to a new unit—the freshly created *Stars and Stripes* daily news publication. The respected newspaper, the *Times of London*, had moved underground and vacated its London offices, making it available for the *Stars and Stripes* military newsroom. It covered diverse topics, including visiting dignitaries and influential people, sporting events, and combat. Rooney's dream of becoming a writer and journalist began.

In February 1943, a group participated in a training program for civilian and military journalists. Rooney and fellow United Press reporter Walter Cronkite, *Stars and Stripes* correspondent Don Hewitt, and Edward R. Murrow were among the class. Rooney was one of eight correspondents trained to fly on bomber missions with the 8th Air Force. They were known as the Writing 69th, and Rooney flew on the second air raid over Germany. He landed on the beaches of Normandy soon after the June 6, 1944, D-Day invasion orchestrated by land, air, and sea forces accompanying the French Seconde Division Blindé into Paris. He covered the battle of St. Lô.

By mere chance, he was the first journalist to reach Ludendorff Railroad Bridge at Remagen, between Koblenz and Bon, Germany, after the United States Combat Command B, 9th Armored Division, captured it on March 7, 1945. That day, the armored infantry fought across the bridge under fierce enemy fire while the Germans attempted to destroy it with demolition charges. Rooney was 20 miles west when he heard the bridge had been captured.

"It was a reporter's dream," he wrote. "One of the great stories of the war had fallen into my lap."

The story hit front-page news in the United States.

Later, Rooney became the first American journalist assigned to report on the Nazi concentration camps. A peace-lover at heart, his views were clouded when he witnessed the brutality of war. It profoundly affected him as a writer and a human being and forced a more realistic view of war and its purpose. Uncovering the widespread death and destruction transformed his ideas of life.

His first book, *Air Gunner*, coauthored with Oram C. "Bud" Hutton in 1944, is based on his eyewitness account of the dramatic and often ghastly experiences as an Army war correspondent. It became a bestseller. Rooney cowrote two more books, *Conquerors' Peace* and *The Story of Stars and Stripes*, with Hutton. In his 1995 memoir *My War*, he chronicled the war, again recounting, firsthand, notable historical events and the people who fought.

In 1945, Rooney, a highly decorated war correspondent, was discharged from the Army. He received the Bronze Star Medal, the fourth-highest ranking award a service member can receive in the US military. It is awarded to recipients who have performed a heroic or meritorious deed in armed conflict. He was also awarded the Air Medal, presented for single acts of heroism or meritorious achievements while participating in aerial flight in support of the operations in combat zones.

Upon discharge, Rooney returned to Albany as a freelance writer. In 1949, he accepted the position as a writer for the radio and television variety show *Arthur Godfrey's Talent Scouts* and *Arthur Godfrey and His Friends*. With Rooney as a writer, *Arthur Godfrey's Talent Scouts* became even more popular; and in 1951, it skyrocketed to the rank of number one. His talent in writing led to Godfrey offering him a position writing for his daytime radio and television show *Arthur Godfrey Time*.

Rooney explained, "After the war, I went to work for radio and television because I didn't think anyone was paying enough attention to the written word."

Rooney adapted E.B. White's essay *Here is New York* for television in 1957, and in 1959, he began writing for a variety series, *The Garry Moore Show*, featuring comedy skits, monologues, and singing. It, too, became a hit program. By the 1960s, he focused on more serious issues. He wrote headline stories for CBS Radio Network, CBS-TV, and CBS News *The 20th Century* and the *Calendar* segment, a live broadcast hosted by Harry Reasoner and Mary Fickett.

Partnering with CBS News correspondent Reasoner, he collaborated on a collection of essays from 1962 to 1968, including *An Essay on Doors* (1964) *An Essay on Bridges* (1965), *An Essay on Hotels* (1966), *An Essay on Women* (1967), *An Essay on Chairs* (1968), and *The Strange Case of the English Language* (1968). He wrote, and Reasoner narrated his text. This essay format, pioneered by Rooney, catapulted him to celebrity.

Rooney contributed two scripts, titled *Of Black America*, to the series *Black History: Lost, Stolen, or Strayed,* narrated by Bill Cosby. It earned Rooney the prestigious Writers Guild Award and his first Emmy Award.

In 1962, Rooney wrote the gripping accounts and actual experiences of World War II soldiers in combat titled *The Fortunes of War Four Great Battles of World War II.*

His 1970 World War II memoir titled *An Essay on War* was written for television broadcast on CBS, but the channel refused to air the controversial essay about the Vietnam War. As a result, Rooney bought the rights to the piece, angrily resigned from his position with CBS, and moved to ABC. He presented the essay on PBS television's *The Great American Dream Machine* in 1971. Notably, it was his first performance presenting his own work in front of the camera. His essay earned him a Writers Guild of America award.

Taking up employment with CBS again in 1973 as a writer and producer of specials, he appeared in broadcasts, including *In Praise of New York City* (1974), *Mr. Rooney Goes to Washington* (1975), which won him a Peabody Award for excellence in broadcasting, *Mr. Rooney Goes to Dinner* (1976), and *Mr. Rooney Goes to Work* (1977).

In 1978, Andy Rooney began his widely popular segment on the CBS newsmagazine *60 Minutes*, a program with a viewership that grew to over seven million people weekly. It was titled *A Few Minutes with Andy Rooney* and offered insight into everyday life and more serious social and political issues. The weekly segment, which aired the final minutes of each program, was initially a replacement for the station's debate segment *Point/Counterpoint*, where two journalists—one liberal, the other conservative—discussed current issues. Rooney's crowd-pleasing commentary became a permanent spot on the program roster. *Point/Counterpoint* was dropped for all time from *60 Minutes*. Amusingly, the *Point/Counterpoint* debate concept was adapted in a recurring comical skit on *Saturday Night Live*, scripted by Dan Akroyd and Jane Curtain.

Andy Rooney was never shy or apprehensive about observing and questioning life's mundane, absurd, ridiculous, and foolish practices and circumstances. He had a distinct talent for straight talk—always being honest. He never sugar-coated his opinions or words. His commentaries included off-the-wall topics like addressing directions that come with new appliances, how to save time, the truth about lying, and his opinion on taking naps, to name a few. He discussed his feelings about sports, entertainment, travel, personal philosophies, and international politics from his wide range of content. He will forever be known for his pessimistic catchphrase known as the 50-50-90 rule—"Anytime you have a 50-50 chance of getting something right, there's a 90 percent probability you'll get it wrong."

In an interview, Rooney confessed feeling deep regret in delivering one of his essays in particular. It involved his unfavorable opinion of the Miss America Pageant and the contestants who represented each state in America. He set out to select an assortment of "homely women," as he termed them, who won the contest over the years. He chose one person from the list, Miss America 1942. He did not realize who she was until he received a sad letter from comedic actor Phil Silvers. She had been his first wife, Jo-Carroll Dennison. It made Rooney feel terrible about the broadcast, saying, "I wish I hadn't done it."

Rooney's tenure with *60 Minutes* remained throughout his career. Each Sunday evening for 33 years, he delighted viewers with his wit and directness, speaking to television audiences from behind his famous walnut table, which he had made himself. His final essay, *My Lucky Life*, aired on October 2, 2011. It was his 1,097th commentary.

"I've done a lot of complaining here," he said of his time with *60 Minutes*, "But of all the things I've complained about, I can't complain. I probably haven't said anything here that you didn't already know or have already thought."

A prolific author, Rooney continued to publish essays throughout his life. His essay compilations can be found in *Pieces of My Mind* (1984), *Sweet and Sour* (1992), *Sincerely, Andy Rooney* (1999), *Common Nonsense* (2002), and *Out of My Mind* (2006), among others.

Andy Rooney won many awards for his essays, including four Emmy Awards—1968, 1979, 1981, and 1982. In 2001, Rooney received the Emperor Has No Clothes Award from the Freedom from Religion Foundation. In 2003, he won a Lifetime Achievement Emmy Award.

Rooney married Marguerite "Margie" Howard in 1942, just before his Army unit left for England. After the war, in 1951, the couple moved to Rowayton, Connecticut, where Margie became a math teacher. The couple were married for 62 years until his wife suffered heart failure and died in 2004. Together, they had four children—Emily, who worked as a TV talk show host and former ABC News producer; her identical twin, Martha Fishel, who became chief of the Public Services Division at the National Library of

Medicine in Bethesda, Maryland; Ellen, a former film editor with ABC News, who worked as a travel and garden photographer based in London; and Brian, a correspondent for ABC.

After Margie's death, Rooney wrote of his late wife, "Her name does not appear as often as it originally did [in my essays] because it hurts too much to write it."

On November 4, 2011, less than five weeks after his last appearance, he died after developing a postoperative complication from an undisclosed surgical procedure. He was 92.

Andy Rooney led an active lifestyle to the end. He was a man of wit and growl, with a heaping dose of common sense, and his candid observations about the things that annoyed him kept viewers engrossed in his weekly commentary.

Summing up his career, Rooney said, "I don't think of myself as a television personality. I'm a writer who reads what I've written. A writer's job is to tell the truth. I have always hoped that people will like what I've written. Being liked is nice, but it's not my intention. I spent my first 50 years trying to become well-known as a writer and the next 30 trying to avoid being famous."

When you endeavor to collaborate on a book such as this, as well as our previous volume of *Words That Shaped Our World*, it is an ongoing challenge to determine who should be included and who should be left out. Then there's the question of what order historical figures and celebrities should appear within the book. Amidst all of this mental struggle, selecting and placing Andy Rooney was simple. He had a ringside seat at some of the most important moments of the 20th century that irrevocably changed the world in which we live. Once it became obvious to us that Andy Rooney had to be included in this book, the placement of his chapter was simple. For several generations of television viewers watching the *60 Minutes* news magazine program, Andy Rooney was literally and figuratively the last word, so it is fitting that we end this book with him.

Mr. Rooney's quote is exemplified by his life—"Most of us end up with no more than five or six people who remember us. Teachers have thousands of people who remember them for the rest of their lives." He took the news of the day or popular cultural trends and taught us about them. When it was all said and done, Andy Rooney didn't offer us his opinion as much as he caused us to contemplate, develop our critical thinking, and formulate our own opinions. He will always be remembered as a reporter who gave us the facts and a teacher who taught us to observe, think, and change our lives.

ABOUT JIM STOVALL

IN SPITE OF BLINDNESS, JIM STOVALL has been a National Olympic weightlifting champion, a successful investment broker, the president of the Emmy Award-winning Narrative Television Network, and a highly sought-after author and platform speaker. He is the author of more than 50 books including the bestseller *The Ultimate Gift*, which is now a major motion picture from 20th Century Fox starring James Garner and Abigail Breslin. Five of his other novels have also been made into movies with two more in production.

Steve Forbes, president and CEO of *Forbes* magazine, says, "Jim Stovall is one of the most extraordinary men of our era."

For his work in making television accessible to our nation's 13 million blind and visually impaired people, the President's Committee on Equal Opportunity selected Jim Stovall as the Entrepreneur of the Year. Jim Stovall has been featured in *The Wall Street Journal,* *Forbes* magazine, *USA Today*, and has been seen on *Good Morning America, CNN,* and *CBS Evening News.* He was also chosen as the International Humanitarian of the Year, joining Jimmy Carter, Nancy Reagan, and Mother Teresa as recipients of this honor.

Jim Stovall can be reached at 918-627-1000 or Jim@JimStovall. com.

ABOUT KATHY JOHNSON

KATHY JOHNSON has been a prominent business writer for many years. She found great success in corporate America with positions of managerial responsibility and charge at various financial institutions developing and directing marketing programs, always maintaining a consistent focus on writing and scripting.

Diversely, she founded and developed several business-to-business magazines, including the regional magazine, *BusinessWise* in Southwest Indiana, serving as owner and editor. Kathy Johnson has edited books, magazines, and articles for various authors, including Jim Stovall.

In addition, she earned her Core Competency and became a Dale Carnegie instructor in relationship, sales, and organizational management.

After completing her academic novella, *Seasons to Remember*, Kathy Johnson earned a Bachelor of Science from the University of Evansville in Evansville, Indiana. She earned a Master's degree from Oakland City University in Oakland City, Indiana, collaborating on research titled, *What Employees Want*.

Leaving corporate America, she pursued her long-time passion for drama, suspense, and romance in her historical novel *Destination Alcatraz*. In 2022, in collaboration with Jim Stovall, *Words that Shaped Our World Volume 1* was released.

Kathy Johnson currently resides in central Minnesota. She can be reached at kathyjohnson@kjjohnson.net.

THANK YOU FOR READING THIS BOOK!

If you found any of the information helpful, please take a few minutes and leave a review on the bookselling platform of your choice.

BONUS GIFT!

Don't forget to sign up to try our newsletter and grab your free personal development ebook here:

soundwisdom.com/classics